Out of the Darkness,

Into the Light

The Powerful Secret of Forgiveness

by
Sylvia McGinnis

DEDICATION

To my husband, Mike, who endured many struggles to prove the awesome power of God, and who encouraged me to write the story so that God would receive the glory.

To my children, Chris and Shawn, and daughter-in-law Teresita, who have lived through the years of testing these principles, and have become, themselves, good forgivers.

To my parents, Oliver and Winifred Tanquary, who laid the foundation of faith for me early in life.

To my brother, Lowell, who was already using many of these principles in his own life long before I began to search them out.

I love you all.

I have read numerous books on forgiveness but this author's book truly captures God's heart of love for us and the forgiven through her personal experiences with the Lord and the Word. This takes us to a far deeper understanding and revelation of the amazing power of forgiveness.

Patti Ammann

I have been privileged to sit under the spout of truth and wisdom that comes through this author from the Lord. Here is that flow from the Father's heart in the written page for all to glean.

Tina Hammock

I can learn so much from the truths this author has expressed in this new book. This will mean, too, reading it often as I have new understanding into the power of forgiveness that she writes about. One thing that stood out for me was our ability to wash others in the sacrificial blood of Christ as we have been, if we are His. The author tells you why and how to do that, and that is just the beginning of learning how to live a life of freedom and non-judgment. This book will be a wonderful resource for my personal library!

Barbara Sullivan

The Powerful Secret of Forgiveness is not just another message about receiving personal freedom by forgiving others, although that freedom is powerful indeed! This book elucidates a powerful message of HOPE for those who believe, for those who seem steadfastly mired in sin and even for the most evil of nations! Read it; pass it on to many! I am! The kingdom of hell will not prevail against it.

Chris Seifert

The author takes on a classic topic with volumes written throughout history. Her unique writing style brings a fresh perspective to an important spiritual condition. Woven into the book are fresh new insights like, "humility is willingness to admit that you may not see the whole picture...". But God does. I encourage you to read, learn and apply these suggestions.

Jack Rothenflue, Director
Commission to Every Nation

Do you feel something is hindering you from receiving the fullness of what the Lord has for you? I have read many books on forgiveness, but I feel that this author has received a deeper revelation, which will give you new insights, freedom from bondage, and lead you into a more intimate relationship with the Lord. I know that it has impacted my life in a powerful way.

Teresa Galloway

A great book about forgiveness, but a fantastic book about extending the redemptive nature of forgiveness through prayer to lost loved ones, resulting in breakthrough for them.

Christopher J. Daniel, M.A.
Christian Counselor (LPC)
Author of "The Little Book-
   Alcoholism, Drug Addiction and
   Recovery Made Simple".

Wonderful book on a difficult subject. A book such as this is long overdue, which gently approaches the subject and leads the reader step by step through the process. The use of the carefully selected scriptures give substance to the subject being presented.

Victor Amman

This book is such a good read! Leaders, intercessors and every believer should read this book. The author is a skilled teacher of THE WORD OF GOD. Her life experiences increase the anointing of revelation in the pages of this treasured read! It settled in my heart in all the right places! Glory!

Cheryl Young Archer
Mannequin Ministry

This book will be a valuable resource for those seeking forgiveness and those needing to forgive. It's inspiring, relevant, and most importantly, full of God's Word.

Susan Frazier

This book is written as an informational book but also as a hands-on tool to walk through learning how and why to forgive. It is a great tool especially because the reader will be able to relate to the author as someone who has had her own struggles with unforgiveness and has reaped the benefits of learning to let go and let God.

Monica Wilhite
Intercessor
Impact Healing Rooms

This is a book everyone should read. It reminds us of the importance of forgiveness. In this book, Sylvia McGinnis shows us the keys of freedom to break the bondage which holds us back from enjoying a life of joy, peace and having a glorious relationship with our Lord God Almighty.

Sherry Greiner
The Coming King Foundation

ACKNOWLEDGEMENTS

I am so very grateful to Ann Sparks for her long hours of help in my previous book as well as this one. Her commitment to seeing people set free from emotional trauma has given me additional incentive to tell this story and reveal the strategy that the Lord has given me. Many thanks also to friends and family who have urged me on. I am grateful to Chris Seifert for her meticulous editing of the manuscript, as well as those who critiqued, made suggestions, and offered endorsements.

My deepest appreciation goes to God the Father, the Son, and Holy Spirit, who stuck with me and tutored me as I learned the real meaning of forgiveness, and then helped me put it into words.

ACKNOWLEDGMENTS

TABLE OF CONTENTS

PREFACE

I have an exciting story to tell! I have seen the mighty works of a great and awesome God! He set me on a path of understanding that untangled my mess, brought order to my thinking, and gave me a spiritual strategy to bring His light into my home and wherever I laid my foot! I have always enjoyed mystery stories. I follow the countless tragedies in the plot, looking for clues that will lead me to the resolution of the problems, where I can say, "Ah-ha! So THAT was what I needed to know! That was the missing piece!" And God allowed me to live a real-life mystery so that He could reveal an answer from scripture that was so simple and so profound that I could not believe I had missed it for years and years.

But let's go back to the beginning. Once upon a time, our home was a place of darkness. Although I knew the Lord, I was filled with discouragement because my husband did not seem interested in the things of God, and this lack of unity played out in our daily lives and the decisions we made, as well as our spiritual and emotional atmosphere. I prayed, I cried out to God for years, and yet, nothing was changing....until the Lord revealed His strategy for breakthrough! That strategy that began with bringing peace into a troubled marriage but then exploded into a much larger picture of the authority of Christian believers in these end times.

What God has done for us He will do for you. In His Word is a truth, a Key to the Kingdom, that will unlock chains of captivity and release people from their spiritual blindness, bringing them into the light!

My prayer for you is that you will read, absorb, apply to your own life, and see the great abundance of blessings that the Lord has for YOU!

Sylvia McGinnis

CHAPTER 1
HAVING DONE ALL... STAND!

Therefore, take up the whole armor of God that you may withstand in the evil day, and having done all......STAND.

Ephesians 6:13

STAND??? Just stand and do nothing? I thought about the years I had invested in praying for my family, especially my husband. We were always in turmoil, but things seemed to be getting worse. Impossible. I'd prayed everything... that he would find happiness, peace, and be able to love and be loved, and that he would seek out the One who could fill that empty place in his heart. That he would want God to be a part of his life. And that this horrible nagging pain in my heart would go away. I had certainly done my best... let him know often that God loved him. I guess that had fallen on deaf ears. Yes, and I had cleverly arranged the usual manipulations like leaving the Bible open on the coffee table, Christian literature in the bathroom, notices of Christian events stuck between papers by his easy chair... and playing praise music, and Christian TV, and yes, I had certainly done it all. Disappointment overwhelmed me. I was tired of fighting. All the things I knew had failed. I was powerless. Hadn't people told me that God never opposes a person's free will? That until that person is ready to submit to God, there is nothing we can do about it? And now the scripture was telling me, *"having done all... STAND".* I guess I just never had enough faith. Just what had caused me to believe that God could get through to him, anyway?

It must have been that promise in Acts 16:31, *"Believe on the Lord Jesus Christ, and you shall be saved, you and your household."* I was so sure that God would be faithful to hear my prayers and do SOMETHING to change my husband. Could it be after all this time, I misunderstood? *"Having done all... STAND".* STAND. Maybe I didn't understand the word *stand.* I grabbed the dictionary.

> *Stand:* to rise to an upright position
> to maintain one's position
> to be firm and steadfast in support or
> opposition
> to endure or undergo successfully
> to tolerate
> to rest or remain upright on a base
> to remain valid or efficacious (having the
> power to produce the desired effect)

An interesting scene was emerging in my mind. Jesus being nailed to the cross. The hostile crowd hovering nearby, oblivious that they were killing the totally innocent, sinless Son of the Living God. Why couldn't they see it? Were they blind? The cross now was being raised to an upright position. Jesus, firm and steadfast in opposition to satan and his works. Jesus, enduring and tolerating the ultimate pain unto death, remaining upright on the base of the cross. Jesus, valid and with power to produce the effect desired by the Father, with blood flowing from His tortured body, crying out, "Forgive them, Father, for they know not what they do!" And the incredible power of God was unleashed to rip the veil of the Holy of Holies in the Temple.

God's statement to mankind was that the debt of all sin had been paid and that we had been divinely forgiven. We were now welcome into the Holy of Holies, the Secret Place, to commune with God the Father. What an amazing concept! Jesus was not just forgiving those present for His torture and manner of death, but He was forgiving every sin of mankind committed from the beginning of time until the end. The blood atonement was now available for ALL of us, just waiting to be applied to and accepted by each individual.

It was available to my husband. I just needed to figure out how he could receive it.

And what about the position I had come to myself? Weak. Powerless. Emotionally drained. Humbled. At the end of myself. Like Jesus?

Most assuredly, I say unto you, unless a grain of wheat falls into the ground and dies, it remains alone; but if it dies, it produces much grain. He who loves his life in this world will lose it; and he who hates his life in this world will keep it for eternal life. If anyone serves Me, let him follow Me, and where I am, there My servant will be also. If anyone serves Me, him My Father will honor.   John 12:24-26

Therefore I take pleasure in infirmities, in reproaches, in needs, in persecutions, in distresses, for Christ's sake. For when I am weak, then I am strong.   II Corinthians 12:10

For though He was crucified in weakness, yet He lives by the power of God. For we also are weak in Him, but we shall live with Him by the power of God toward you. II Corinthians 13:4

A ray of light was beginning to dawn. MY strength was ebbing away, but God was replacing it with the strength of His Spirit. I would STAND, alright, in HIS power, and HE would receive the glory, not I! As a broken vessel, I agreed, "Do it YOUR way, Lord. Be it unto me according to Your word. But... I'm trusting in You. Please bring my husband into the light of Your Kingdom!"

Rise and stand on your feet; for I have appeared to you for this purpose, to make you a minister and a witness both of the things which you have seen and of the things which I will yet reveal to you. I will deliver you from the Jewish people, as well as the Gentiles, to whom I now send you, to open their eyes and turn them from darkness to light, and from the power of Satan to God, that they may receive forgiveness of sins and an inheritance among those who are sanctified by faith in Me.

Acts 26:16-18

CHAPTER 2

THE PROBLEM OF SPIRITUAL BLINDNESS

Can you remember a time when you felt that God had touched you or a time when you felt particularly blessed by God? Once that has happened to you, it becomes difficult to understand others who reject God as fiction and cannot believe that He is there for them. There is a "blindness" to the incredible love and power that is available to them, and they go through life having to face struggles on their own.

Because of the vision I had experienced as I read the dictionary definition of *stand,* I decided to look up *blind.*

blind: *sightless*
         unable or unwilling to discern or judge
         having no regard to rational discrimination,
             guidance, or restriction
         lacking any directing or controlling
             consciousness
         marked by complete insensibility
         hidden from sight; covered
         having no opening for light or passage

Yes, I could see many people without God in their lives having some of these characteristics. I asked, "What causes people to be blind to God?"

THE CAUSE OF SPIRITUAL BLINDNESS

Let's take a look at three short scriptures.

> *But your iniquities have separated you from your God; and your sins have hidden His face from you so that He will not hear. Isaiah 59:2*

> *Woe to us for we have sinned. Because of this our hearts are faint and sick; our eyes are dim and see darkly. Lamentations 5:16-17*

> *But he who hates his brother is in darkness and walks in darkness, and does not know where he is going, because the darkness has blinded his eyes. I John 2:11*

In the first scripture we see that *iniquities* cause a separation or a division between ourselves and God. The word *iniquity*, as defined in the Hebrew language, means perversity or moral evil that has been passed from generation to generation down the family line. It is sin that has not been forgiven. That scripture also tells us that our own sin *has hidden His face* and that God *will not hear*. In other words, sin becomes a barrier between ourselves and God. It is not that God wants to separate Himself from us, it is that sin itself becomes a barrier between us.

Lamentations 5: 16-17 shows us the result of being separated from God. *Our hearts are faint and sick; our eyes are dim and see darkly.* And I John 2:11 indicates that hate, being a sin that separates us from God, leaves us blind and without guidance.

Well, then, if sin is the cause of spiritual blindness, then removing that barrier of sin should take care of the problem! The important question becomes, how is a barrier of sin removed? The Word of God says,

> *Repent, then, and be converted, that your sins may be blotted out, so that times of refreshing may come from the Lord. Acts 3:19*

That sounds simple... but wait a minute! The spiritually blind people I know don't believe that they have any sin, so it wouldn't even dawn on them to repent! This barrier not only blinds them from God, it blinds them from their own sin. Iniquity that has come down the generations causes people to behave in ways that bring negative reactions from others. Those negative reactions leave our blind persons with emotional woundings. Out of their woundedness they become hard to get along with but view their relationship problems as the fault of others. They may be demanding and pushy, or withdrawing and uncommunicative. They may work hard to preserve some relationships out of fear for their jobs or fear of being alone, but without a genuine love flowing from God they "give out" in time. A false love that is manufactured from the flesh loses energy quickly. There is an emptiness within them in that beautiful place God created for His Spirit alone. It is only God who is able to reveal the sin problem in the heart of a soul separated from Him. Daniel 2:22 says of God,

> *He reveals deep and secret things; He knows what is in the darkness, and light dwells with Him.*

So if they need God to see their own sin, and they cannot see God because of the barrier that separates them from God, has God provided a way out of this CATCH-22? YES!!! God has made provision for our spiritually blind loved ones from the very beginning!

THE BARRIER OF SIN REMOVED

> *I will bring the blind by a way they did not know; I will lead them in paths they have not known. I will make darkness light before them, and crooked places straight. These things I will do for them and not forsake them. Isaiah 42:16*

I was greatly relieved to know that the Lord already had a working plan! From the time of the Garden of Eden in Genesis, when sin entered the world bringing blindness and spiritual death, God countered the effect of that by paying for death with a life, and the life was in the shedding of blood. God shed the blood of an animal to atone for the sin of Adam and Eve, and He wrapped them in its skin. Animal sacrifice became an important part of Hebrew worship as a means of "covering" sin and removing its barrier temporarily. The scripture tells us in Hebrews 9:7,

> *But into the second part of the Temple (the Holy of Holies) the High Priest went alone once a year, not without blood, which he offered for himself and for the people's sins committed in ignorance.*

This was a temporary procedure performed over and over again until the permanent solution became operational. God came to earth Himself in the form of the sinless Jesus Christ to become both the High Priest and the sacrificial Lamb of God. He gave His own blood, paying the debt for our sins, as a one-time-for-all sacrifice. Never again would animals have to be killed for this purpose. The power of His blood would be available to every person on Planet Earth to tear down the barrier of sin. Each person could be forgiven and offered fellowship with Father God. Fellowship with God meant that prayers would be heard and answered, and that every person could receive healing and protection, provision and guidance. Every person could become a pipeline of God's love to the world, and every bit of territory taken by satan at the

Fall of Man could be restored. What takes away that barrier of sin? Sing along with me:

What can wash away my sin?

Nothing but the blood of Jesus!

In this book we will learn how to apply the shed blood of Jesus Christ for our own sin and the sins of others also, so that we are forgiven and they are, too!

THE BLESSINGS OF BEING FORGIVEN

As you can see, there are huge benefits in being forgiven and having an open heaven! Let's examine four scriptural passages about what occurs when people are forgiven.

1. THEY ARE BLESSED. (The Amplified Bible defines *blessed* as *happy, fortunate, to be envied, spiritually prosperous, with life-joy and satisfaction in God's favor and salvation.*)

    Blessed are those whose lawless deeds are forgiven, and whose sins are covered. (Psalms 32:1-2) Blessed is the man to whom the Lord shall not impute sin. (Romans 4:7-8.)

2. THEY RECEIVE REVELATION OF GOD.

    Fear not, for I have redeemed you; I have called you by your name. For I am the Lord your God, the Holy One of Israel, your Savior.

Bring out the blind people who have eyes, and the deaf who have ears. You are My witnesses, says the Lord, and My servants whom I have chosen, that you may know and believe Me, and understand that I am He. Before Me there was no God formed, nor shall there be after Me. I, even I am the Lord and besides Me there is no savior. Isaiah 43:1, 3, 8, 10, 11

3. THEY RECEIVE REVELATION OF THEIR NEED FOR REPENTANCE, A SPIRITUAL REFRESHING, AND REVELATION OF JESUS CHRIST.

Repent, then, and be converted, that your sins may be blotted out, so that times of refreshing may come from the presence of the Lord and that He may send Jesus Christ who was preached to you before. Acts 3:19-20

4. THEY WILL BE FREE TO LOVE.

In the Book of Luke there is a story about a sinful woman who anointed the feet of Jesus with a very expensive oil, exhibiting her great love for Him. In explaining to those present His approval of her actions, Jesus said, *Therefore I say to you, her sins, which are many, are forgiven, for she loved much. But to whom little is forgiven, the same loves little. Luke 7:47.* In other words, she would not have been able to love in such a selfless and sacrificial way if God's love had not been flowing through her, and that only happens when a person has been forgiven. Forgiveness, then, frees us from those things that keep us from loving with a God-like love. Do you know people who seem to not be able to love? They need forgiveness!

CHRISTIANS CAN ALSO HAVE A BARRIER OF SIN

Those who have not invited the Lord into their hearts are not the only ones who are spiritually blind. The word sin is defined in the Greek to *miss the mark* of God's perfect will. As human beings, we often miss the bullseye of God's plan for us, acting out of our emotions and unsanctified souls. Thank God that He is always faithful to continue His work in us. But while we are under construction we need to go boldly to the Throne of Grace on a daily basis, asking forgiveness for our sins, known and unknown. Failure to own up to our weaknesses and accept the blood remission of our sins will take us into a state of spiritual blindness and hardness of heart. Like David in the Old Testament, we need to say humbly, *Create in me a clean heart, oh God (Psalms 51:10)* and allow the Lord opportunity to show us areas of our lives that need cleansing.

There are many sins that set up a barrier of spiritual blindness. In this book, we will focus on one particular sin that covertly sneaks into our everyday lives, erecting that barrier without immediate detection! This is the sin that tripped me up for so many years and stole so much of my life. It is a sin that is rampant in the body of Christ. It tears relationships apart. It tears churches apart. It dangerously hinders the work of Christ in the world. It is satan's strategy to steal, kill, and destroy.

IT IS THE SIN OF JUDGMENT.

Matthew 7:1 tells us: *Judge not, that you be not judged.* Because this admonition is a commandment of God, we are in sin when we judge others, and this sin presents a barrier to communication with God. Whenever a Christian complains to me, "I don't know what's wrong. I just don't feel like my prayers are going anywhere. I feel so far away from God", I ask, "Has someone hurt you recently?" Usually that person is holding a judgment on someone who has been unkind, and it has cut off his communication with the Lord.

The reason judgment is such a serious sin is that *holding* someone in judgment keeps that person a prisoner in the spiritual realm if they have sinned. They are separated from God's blessings. And we become prisoners also because of our sin of holding them in judgment. If this statement seems a little harsh to you, go to Matthew 18:21-35 in your Bible.

I will summarize that story. Jesus instructs Peter to forgive seventy times seven times; in other words, there is no limit to the amount of times you must forgive. He then relates a parable of a servant who owed his master a great debt that he could not afford to pay. Out of compassion, the master cancelled the debt and set him free. But later, that servant went out to a fellow servant who owed him money and had him thrown into prison when he couldn't repay. He could have "forgiven" the debt, but he chose instead to keep the man in bondage. When the master heard this, he was furious, and had the original servant thrown into prison, too. Jesus ends by saying, *So My heavenly Father also will do to you if each of you, from his heart, does not forgive his brother his trespasses.*

Of course, if a person has no "debt" (sin), my judgment cannot hold him in bondage. It takes humility to understand that there are times that we feel hurt by another person when they actually did nothing to try to hurt us! Because of woundedness we have suffered in the past, we may **perceive** that a person in the present is being rude or offensive or has evil motives when that is not the case at all! Later in the book we will discuss the effects of woundedness and how to deal with our hurts and trauma from the past.

But if a person HAS sinned and I have the key of forgiveness in my hand and the power to set him free and I REFUSE TO DO SO, then I am guilty of the sin of judgment and I am now in spiritual bondage, unable to receive revelation or blessing from God. This is serious business! One problem is that when someone hurts us, we don't really think of it as a "debt" owed to us, so we don't recognize our own tendency to extract payment from that person by a "silent retaliation" in our mind. We build anger, resentment and bitterness by "playing tapes" in our head, replaying the scenario. We give them "a piece of our mind", not out loud, but nevertheless in a brutal, negative way inwardly. We think we can get by with this "silent retaliation", but we are only hurting ourselves. Carrie Fisher, the famous Star Wars heroine, is quoted as saying, *Resentment is like drinking poison and expecting the other person to die.* Hateful words, whether thought or spoken aloud, are physically damaging. And thoughts and words of judgment erect a barrier of sin that causes us to be spiritually blind.

Let me give a fictional example of how easy it is for perfectly nice people to fall into spiritual blindness.

A man named Tom gets up on the wrong side of the bed one morning and says something rude to his wife, Judy. He has started his day by sinning. He knows he needs to apologize to his wife and to the Lord, but his pride keeps him from doing so. Judy is hurt and offended. She mentally self-protects, lashes back in her mind, and judges him in her thoughts. She has sinned and now is in blindness, too. Since both parties are separated from God's love and power, there is very little chance of reconciling words. Judy turns a cold shoulder to Tom as he leaves for work and makes a sarcastic remark. Tom is hurt and offended. The barrier is reinforced.

During the day, Judy calls a friend and tells her how unkind Tom is. Her friend forms a judgment on Tom, picks up Judy's offence and now she is in spiritual darkness also. If she spreads the word to others about Tom, they will join her and Judy in the spiritual dungeon.

At the office, Tom looks for sympathy for his wounded ego, which his young secretary is happy to provide... and on the story goes. The sad part is that each party in this story feels justified in his judgment, and no one is humble enough to break this contagious disease, therefore all are losing their blessings.

How could this chain reaction have been avoided? Tom might have been humble enough to ask for forgiveness at the beginning. But if he did not, Judy could have been humble enough to forgive him immediately. In fact, if Judy had done that and released him from his darkness, Tom might have received revelation from God about his own sin and apologized! If she had forgiven and he had still not faced his sin, at least SHE would have been free of spiritual bondage and able to keep seeking God's help and guidance for him.

TWO KINDS OF JUDGMENT

You may be saying right now, "But as a Christian, aren't I called to judge certain situations?" Yes!! Let's review I Corinthians 2:15-16.

> But he who is spiritual judges all things, yet he himself is rightly judged by no one. For "who has known the mind of the Lord that he may instruct Him"? But we have the mind of Christ.

In this scripture the Greek word for "judge" is *anakrino*, which means "*to scrutinize, investigate, interrogate, determine, ask, question, discern, examine, and search*". In other words, we are to understand what is going on.

But in Matthew 7:1, where we are commanded not to "judge", the Greek word is *krino*, which means "*to try, condemn, damn, decree, go to the law.*" That word is also related to the word *krisis* which means "*accusation, condemnation, and damnation.*" The first type of judgment is simply informational. But the judgment we are discussing in this book is *krino*. It is accompanied by negative emotional involvement and a desire for revenge. While we, as Christians, have the mind of Christ to *anakrino*, we do not have the right to *krino*, because we do not have all the facts that God has in order to administer justice. The two scriptures are not contradictory. We are to make careful evaluation of every situation. Then, if offense is involved, we are to release the offenders, through forgiveness, to the Lord for His perfect judgment.

ONE NATION UNDER DARKNESS

Our nation has become a nation of judgment. The media encourages us constantly to "have an opinion". Talk shows and tabloids stir up controversy and strife, both being judgmental. The evening news is an incubator of sensationalism, designed to enflame public opinion. Public accusations and slander incite violence and lawsuits, and blame is spewed over prosecutors, judges, lawyers, juries... the result is a total darkness over our justice system. Our national and state leaders are under constant criticism, even by Christians! We judge our pastors, our bosses, our neighbors. The more we judge, the more confusion reigns as the barrier grows thicker, hiding God's face. And all the while, those leaders desperately need the light of God in order to do their jobs well! No wonder the Lord has told us not to judge, but to pray for the leaders who are over us. As we use the "key of forgiveness" to set them free from darkness, they can receive the wisdom of God to make good decisions, and we will be blessed!

Therefore I exhort first of all that supplications, prayers, and giving of thanks be made for all men, for kings and all who are in authority, that we may lead a quiet and peaceable life in all godliness and reverence. For this is good and acceptable in the sight of God our Savior, who desires all men to be saved and come to the knowledge of the truth.
I Timothy 2: 1-4

Joseph L. Garlington, senior pastor of Covenant Church in Pittsburgh in 1994, recalled a moment of anger in his life in which he judged some senators for their actions. He is quoted as saying, *"It was in my moment of righteous disapproval that the Holy Spirit responded, 'You cannot be an authentic intercessor if you count any man's sins against him'. I knew immediately the privilege of serving God as an intercessor does not include the authority to judge at the same time....I learned a key principle of intercession: You cannot judge with one hand and extend mercy with the other."*

Oh, my. The words "righteous disapproval" caught my eye. Looking back on the years I had thought I was interceding for my husband, I wondered if I had ever really been an "authentic" intercessor. Mostly, I had begged the Lord to bring him into the Kingdom...but not for his sake... for mine. I thought that if he was a Christian, he would make my life easier. And all the while, I complained with "righteous disapproval" about what I wanted God to change in my husband. Humbly, I admitted that my motives were terrible, my attitude was self-righteous and prideful, and that I was the one that needed the change. I asked God to forgive me.

I am still amazed at what happened in the wake of that prayer. The barrier that I hadn't even known was there, came down. The scriptures came alive to me as God revealed the role of forgiveness in opening blind eyes. The revelation began with a phone call.

CHAPTER 3

OPENING THE EYES OF THE BLIND

The voice of my friend on the phone asked, "Sylvia, what is the Spirit of Elijah?" I hadn't the slightest idea. It was worth pursuing, so I turned to I Kings 18 and began to read the story of Elijah and the prophets of Baal. Here is a short summary.

There was great idolatry in Israel. Elijah the prophet had confronted King Ahab and ordered him to bring the prophets of the "gods" Baal and Asherah and all of the Israelites to Mount Carmel. There they would carry out an experiment to discover which god, Baal or the Lord God Jehovah, was the *true* God. The Israelites were double-minded; when Elijah asked them to make up their minds whom they would worship, they were silent. They truly did not know, because they were blinded by their iniquities. So, at Elijah's suggestion (which was surely the Lord's idea!) the prophets of Baal put up an altar with a sacrifice to their god and called for Baal to send down fire from heaven to consume it. Of course, nothing happened! Elijah then called the people to come close to him. He built an altar to the Lord and put upon it wood and a sacrifice, and then poured water all around it and over it three times.

> *And it came to pass, at the time of the offering of the evening sacrifice, that Elijah the*

prophet came near and said, "Lord God of Abraham, Isaac, and Israel, let it be known this day that You are the Lord God, and that You have turned their hearts back to you again." Then the fire of the Lord fell and consumed the burnt sacrifice, and the wood and the stones and the dust, and it licked up the water that was in the trench. Now when all the people saw it, they fell on their faces; and they said "The Lord, He is God! The Lord, He is God!" I Kings 18:36-39

Perhaps you would think that physically seeing fire fall from heaven was enough to convince the confused Israelites. But interestingly, if you have had any experience with spiritually blind people, you know that they will not accept even signs and wonders that show the power of God. Because of unbelief, skepticism, and fear they will readily explain away any miracle with elaborate scientific theories rather than admit the presence of a supernatural God. However, the scripture says *they fell on their faces* in an act of repentance and submission. THE SACRIFICE CONSUMED ON THE ALTAR PROVIDED FOR THE ATONEMENT OF THEIR SIN. The Lord, in essence, declared by fire from heaven that the sacrifice was acceptable and that their sin had been fully forgiven! The barrier was down! Without that barrier of sin to blind them from God, they became aware of their own sinfulness and had a revelation of the identity of the true Lord God.

Elijah's prayer, *that You have turned their hearts back to You again,* clearly tells us that it is the LORD'S RESPONSIBILITY to do the work of changing their hearts. Elijah's responsibility was simply to provide the setting that was needed to do the work: an altar of worship, the wood (symbolic of the cross to be revealed later), the sacrifice (symbolic of Jesus the Messiah, the Lamb of God, and the blood He shed) and the water (symbolic of the Word of God). The Lord's response, fire from heaven (symbolic of the Holy Spirit) completed the atonement for sin and set them free from spiritual blindness.

TURNING HEARTS TO GOD BY THE POWER OF THE SPIRIT OF ELIJAH

The Word of the Lord in prophesy tells us that Elijah will *come again* before the coming of the Messiah.

> *Behold, I will send you Elijah the prophet before the coming of the great and dreadful day of the Lord. And he will turn the hearts of the fathers to the children, and the hearts of the children to the fathers, lest I come and strike the earth with a curse.   Malachi 4:5-6*

"Turning the hearts of the fathers to the children" sounds very familiar, doesn't it? We just read Elijah's prayer to *turn their hearts back to You again.* God the Father is again taking total responsibility for changing the hearts of His children and drawing them to Him. How did He plan to do this? By bringing a special man into the world with the same spirit as the prophet Elijah. He would prepare the way for the Messiah by removing the barrier of sin so that the people would recognize the Messiah as the Man of God.

His name was John the Baptist. In this passage, God the Father is speaking through the prophet to His Son, Jesus Christ, introducing Him to His cousin, John the Baptist. And God is also speaking to us.

> *For this is he of whom it is written, "Behold I send My messenger before Your face, who will prepare Your way before You." And if you are willing to receive it, he is Elijah who is to come. He who has ears, let him hear!*
> *Matthew 11:10, 14-15*

> *The voice of one crying in the wilderness; prepare the way of the Lord; make straight in the desert a highway for our God. And the Glory of the Lord shall be revealed.*
> *Isaiah 40: 3-5*

The angel of the Lord came to announce the miracle of this child's conception to Elizabeth, John's mother-to-be, who had aged long beyond child-bearing years. He spoke these words to her.

And he will turn many of the children of Israel to their God. He will also go before Him [the Messiah] in the spirit and power of Elijah to turn the heart of the fathers to the children, and the disobedient to the wisdom of the just, to make ready a people prepared for the Lord. Luke 1: 16-17

And the father of John the Baptist, Zacharias, prophesied to his son with these words,

And you, child, will be called the prophet of the Highest; for you will go before the face of the Lord to prepare His ways, to give knowledge of salvation to His people by the **remission of their sins**. *Through the tender mercy of our God, with which the Dayspring from on high has visited us;* **to give light to those who sit in darkness and the shadow of death**, *to guide our feet into the way of peace. Luke 1: 76-79*

DIVINE POWER TO BRING REPENTANCE

John the Baptist was equipped from the start with something that no one else had! When the angel spoke to Elizabeth about the impending birth of her son, he said,

He will also be filled with the Holy Spirit, even from his mother's womb. Luke 1:15

With the authority and anointing of the Holy Spirit within him, John the Baptist brought about the remission of sin. Wait a minute… the Old Testament speaks of the *atonement* for sin. The Hebrew word for *atonement* is *"cover"*. The sacrifice of animals "covered" the sin of the people. It was a temporary fix. But now, under the new Covenant that the Messiah would make with the people, the Word speaks of *remission of sin.* The Greek word for *remission* means *"disappear, pardoned, freedom, deliverance".* Remission is PERMANENT. Sins are not just covered; they are GONE! Even before Jesus shed His blood for us in the natural, His covenant was already in operation through John the Baptist. He would *give knowledge of salvation to His people* **by the remission of their sins***.*

John was a pure vessel of the Spirit of God. The Spirit drew the multitudes to him. The love and forgiveness of God overshadowed them. As he urged them to repent and be baptized, the barrier of sin came down and their eyes were opened. They were ready to receive the Messiah when He walked into the picture. God revealed the answer to our question, "What is the Spirit of Elijah?" It is a spirit of love, forgiveness and truth that opens blind eyes and brings in repentance and revelation.

> *And he went into all the region around the Jordan, preaching a baptism of repentance for the remission of sins. Luke 3:3*

*The next day John saw Jesus coming toward him, and said, "Behold! The Lamb of God that takes away the sins of the world! This is He of whom I said, 'After me comes a man who is preferred before me for He was before me. I did not know Him; **but that He should be revealed to Israel, therefore I came baptizing with water'."** And John bore witness, saying, "I saw the Spirit descending from heaven like a dove, and He remained upon Him. I did not know Him, but He who sent me to baptize with water said to me, 'Upon whom you see the Spirit descending, and remaining on Him, this is He who baptizes with the Holy Spirit'. And I have seen and testified that this is the Son of God."*
John 1:25-34

Look at the bold print. This is saying that if John had not come baptizing with water, Jesus would not have been revealed to Israel! Baptism with water was not the main issue here. Receiving water baptism was a sign of obedience that came from a heart that was changed by the revelation of God. The heart can only be changed when there is a revelation of sin followed by repentance. Again we see **the remission of sin clearing the way in men's hearts and minds to receive revelation of the Lord.**

Amazingly enough, even Jesus was baptized by John. Although He was sinless and certainly did not need forgiveness, He stood as an example of humility to all of us, and the baptism opened to Him the fullness of the glory of God to empower Him for ministry of His own in the authority of the Holy Spirit.

> *Then Jesus came from Galilee to John at the Jordan to be baptized by him. And John tried to prevent Him, saying, "I have need to be baptized by You, and are You coming to me?" But Jesus answered and said to him, "Permit it to be so now, for thus it is fitting for us to fulfill all righteousness." Then he allowed Him. Then Jesus, when He had been baptized, came up immediately from the water; and behold, the heavens were opened to Him, and He saw the Spirit of God descending like a dove and alighting upon Him. And suddenly a voice came from heaven, saying, "This is My beloved Son, in whom I am well pleased."*
> *Luke 3: 13-17*

What happened when the multitudes were baptized with the baptism of repentance by John? They became spiritually aware of the presence of God operating in Jesus! In Luke 7, Jesus explained to them why it was that John the Baptist had preceded Him, and as He spoke the people received spiritual understanding.

And when all the people heard Him, even the tax collectors justified God, having been baptized with the baptism of John. But the Pharisees and lawyers rejected the counsel of God for themselves, not having been baptized by him. Luke 7: 29-30

In other words, the Pharisees **had received the counsel of God,** but had rejected the truth because they did not desire to humble themselves in the baptism of repentance in front of the people! But they had experienced the same glimmer of understanding that the multitudes had received about their own sin and had been admonished to repent, yet had chosen out of pride to reject what God was offering....the remission of their sin! Therefore, God allowed their hard hearts to continue in blindness, and they did not recognize Jesus as the Messiah. Power and position were the gods they served, and the Lord gave them free choice.

DIVINE POWER FOR HEALING

Throughout the gospel we see something else happening that is a result of the forgiveness of sin. Jesus is healing and restoring physical bodies! How do we know that this has any relationship with forgiveness? Look at Matthew 9:6 where Jesus is speaking to the paralytic.

But that you may know that the Son of Man
has power on earth to forgive sins, arise, take
up your bed, and go to your house.

In other words He might have said, "If I did not have the power to forgive your sins, you would not be healed". Again, we see the "barrier" of sin being removed by forgiveness and the person being set free to receive the awesome power of God in their life. Sin, then, is a barrier that prevents healing.

Several years ago I knew a woman who was diagnosed with a Stage 4 cancer. A huge inoperable tumor protruded from her abdomen. No longer able to eat, the doctors put her on intravenous fluids for sustenance at her home. The medical community gave her no chance of survival. However, we began a prayer group and Bible Study at her home. We studied Forgiveness, and laid hands on the tumor. She began to forgive the people who had hurt her in her life, and as she released them and we prayed, we saw that tumor shrink until it was gone! Against doctor's orders, she began to eat...and the food went through and was digested! Soon she was feeling good, dressing up in her high heeled shoes and shopping at Walmart! It was a true miracle that proved the power of God to all of her friends and family.

During her traumatic illness she had written to her sister in a foreign country, begging her to come because she thought she was going to die. The sister arrived, but not until she was feeling healthy and looking marvelous…and the sister got extremely angry and accused her of lying about the illness to manipulate her to come. The sister got plane reservations and left the next week. My friend was devastated, and very hurt, angry, bitter, resentful, and….unforgiving. She just couldn't let go and take her judgment off her sister. Over the next few weeks, her energy declined, the tumor grew back, and she died. Forgiveness is not just doing what is right….it may be a matter of life or death to those who need healing.

Consider another scripture about divine healing, Matthew 8:1-3.

> *And behold, a leper came and worshipped Him [Jesus], saying, "Lord, if You are willing, You can make me clean." Then Jesus put out His hand and touched him saying, "I am willing; be cleansed." And immediately his leprosy was cleansed.*

Perhaps we have a play on words here, but the leper was obviously "cleansed" of his sin, and therefore, "cleansed" of his leprosy.

Also, in John 9:7, Jesus said to the blind man, *"Go wash in the pool of Siloam,"* so he went and washed and came back seeing. Again, the words have double meaning, as the "washing" symbolized the baptism of repentance, forgiveness of sin, and the miraculous result of divine healing.

I am a volunteer chaplain for our county jail, and I minister to women who have lived very painful lives. Emotional healing, however, is certainly no more difficult to the Lord than physical healing, if the person is willing to forgive those that have hurt them and also forgive themselves so that healing may begin. One day I came upon a woman who was within two weeks of release from jail. She said sadly, "I should be excited, but I'm really scared. Here in the jail I can't get drugs. But I know what will happen when I hit the street. The addiction is still in me." I knew that the reason she was a prisoner to her addiction was that the agony in her soul from past hurts was so intense that she needed an "anesthetic" to dull the pain. What she really needed was a touch from the Lord to heal her woundedness, and deliverance from addiction. I did not have the time to work through all of her problems with her, so I suggested that she spend the next week asking the Lord to show her all of the people in her life who had caused her pain, to make a written list, and then, one by one, lift each name to the Lord and say, "I *am releasing this person to You, Lord. I am taking my judgment off him so that You can judge him with Your perfect judgment. I forgive him by an act of my will, not my emotions, and set him free.*" I encouraged her also to remember to forgive herself and to give herself over to the Lord just like the others!

My intent was to get her started in the process of healing. When I came again I would work on the deliverance part.

The following week I returned to find her jumping with joy! When she had completed her forgiveness list, she was immediately released from the addiction, and no additional ministry was required! Spiritually, I believe that while she was stuck in the sin of unforgiveness (judgment), satan had "legal right" to bind her in addiction. Forgiving removed the sin barrier and opened her soul to God, while closing the access doors to the devil! The Lord had just been waiting for the opportunity to come in and heal.

SUMMARY

Great blessings come to those who are forgiven of their sins. Sin is the barrier that keeps out the power of God. Judgment (unforgiveness) keeps that barrier in place. But when we forgive and are forgiven and that barrier is removed, we are free to receive:
revelation,
inspiration,
wisdom,
understanding,
refreshing,
provision
guidance,
protection,
the ability to love others,
and healing!

What great riches are in store for us when we are willing to come humbly before the Lord and ask for forgiveness daily as each need arises! And what wonderful changes are in store for those whom we forgive by the power of the Holy Spirit in us.

I would like to clarify here. The **only** power we have to forgive is through the Holy Spirit. If you are reading this book and have not prayed to receive the Holy Spirit of Jesus Christ into your spirit, here is your opportunity! This entire book is about the authority you hold in the spirit realm *if* you have the Holy Spirit.

So I invite you to open your heart and pray this prayer right now and step into God's Kingdom of Light and Love as His beloved child, and enter the world of supernatural blessing!

Lord, I come to You humbly, wanting to become a part of Your mighty work on the earth. There are many things that I have done wrong, but I thank You for the blood You shed on the cross to pay for my sins. I ask Your forgiveness and accept Your blood washing me clean. I ask You to live in me, Holy Spirit. Come in now! You are welcome here! I give over my life to You, that You will use me for heaven's purposes, and fill me with Your love and joy and peace. I pray this in Jesus' precious name, amen.

Now you are ready to begin the forgiveness strategy! Perhaps there is someone you love who is troubled and difficult and needs the help of the Lord. Is it true that you can "forgive" them into the Kingdom of God? Yes!!! Start with the **Forgiveness Prayers** written in the **Appendix**. Forgiveness is a **KEY OF THE KINGDOM.**

CHAPTER 4
A KEY OF THE KINGDOM

For just a minute, allow your mind's eye to return again to the scene at Golgotha, where Jesus was not only "standing", but bleeding and dying a slow, tortuous death on the cross. He was the sinless sacrifice that was acceptable to God for payment of the sin-debt of mankind.

> *For He made Him who knew no sin to be sin for us, that we might become the righteousness of God in Him.*
> *II Corinthians 5:21*

The sin of the world flooded Him, covered Him, surrounded Him. For the first time, the darkness separated Him from His Father, and He cried out,

> *My God, My God, why hast thou forsaken Me?*
> *Matthew 27:46*

Even separation from the Father was not enough to deter the Son from fulfilling His purpose.

> *Forgive them, Father, for they know not what they do. Luke 23:34*

Forgive them! Every sin committed by man from the beginning to the end of time! The blood sacrifice shed for the remission of individual sin, the sin of families, corporate sin, the sin of nations, the sin of cultures and ideologies. A key to unlock chains of darkness and free men of their evil bondages. That key ripped open the veil of the temple at the entrance to the Holy of Holies, opening the throne of God to common man to fellowship with Father God just as Jesus did!

At the scene of the cross, because of the remission of sin, spiritual eyes were opened.

> *Now when the centurion who stood opposite Him saw that He cried out like this and breathed His last, he said, "Truly the Man was the Son of God!" Mark 15:39*

> *And the whole crowd who came together to that sight, seeing what had been done, beat their breasts and returned. Luke 23:48*

Their eyes were opened. Forgiven for their sin, they were not blind to their sin anymore. They knew the truth.

We, too, have been given the keys of the kingdom. Unforgiveness is a power that binds and holds men captive. Forgiveness is a key that looses men from bonds of iniquity. In Matthew 16:19 Jesus said,

> *And I will give you the keys of the kingdom of heaven, and whatever you bind on earth will be bound in heaven, and whatever you loose on earth will be loosed in heaven.*

EXTERMINATING THE EVIL

The apostle Paul, or Saul, as he was called before his conversion, was a man bound to a faulty belief system. He persecuted Christians of the early church because, in his spiritual blindness, he thought he was doing God a favor! In Acts 7, Saul promoted and attended the stoning of Stephen, an early believer. He condoned the torturous death and was therefore guilty of that sin. Stephen, near death, saw Jesus standing at the right hand of God in a vision and cried out, *Lord, do not charge them with this sin!* It was a statement of complete forgiveness.

In Acts 8, Saul became even more contemptible, dragging Christian men and women off to prison with a vengeance. It could be that even then, in the period following the forgiveness of Stephen, he was beginning to get a revelation of his own sin, which only infuriated him more! When people discover that they have believed lies and have built their lives upon those lies, it makes them angry. I call it "backlash". But it is a most important step, and it means that freedom is just around the corner! Have you ever seen a snake with its head cut off? The decapitated body thrashes wildly about until its energy is spent and it collapses. So it was with Saul until he collapsed in Acts 9 on the Damascus Road with a complete revelation of the identity of Jesus Christ, the resurrected Son of God. In my opinion, this revelation was the direct result of the forgiveness of Stephen which removed the barrier of sin between Saul and his God. Stephen had been given the key of forgiveness to open the kingdom of heaven for Saul.

One day I attended a prayer group of very spiritually aggressive mothers who were warring in the Spirit for their difficult children. We prayed forgiveness over each child and asked the Lord to reveal to them the sin in their lives so that they might repent and receive guidance and blessing from God. That evening it appeared that in several homes the behavior of the children was **worse** rather than better. I got a phone call from a friend that night, and told her how confused I was over this, because I had thought that our prayer time was very effective. She said to me, *"The bug exterminator came to my house today and did a really thorough job. He told me that this evening, as the treatment took effect, I would begin to see the roaches crawling out of the woodwork. But not to worry...they'd be real SICK roaches!"* Yes! Things often get worse before they get better when we are routing out the evil of men's hearts. This backlash is to be expected, since people do not like to see the truth about themselves in revelation. Like Saul, they become irritable and difficult until the fullness of the revelation breaks their rebellious spirit and brings repentance.

I was speaking to a friend one day whose husband had recently left her for an unknown reason. He seemed to be so angry and confused about his own life that he chose to blame her and retaliate against her. She was taking it remarkably well, forgiving and standing in prayer for his healing. I said to her, *"How are you able to do this without getting caught up in your own hurt?"*

She replied, "I am seeing him as a prisoner of war. If he was in the army and was taken prisoner, I wouldn't be mad at him, I would pray for him to be released! He has been taken prisoner by the enemy of his soul. I will keep forgiving until he is set free!"

What a victorious attitude! It helps to remember that we are using forgiveness and love as weapons to counter the enemy who is causing the ungodly behavior that is being unleashed. As much as our flesh may want to judge and unload anger and resentment on the "unlovely" person in question, Romans 2:3-4 tells us,

> *And do you think this, O man, you who judge those practicing such things, and doing the same, that you will escape the judgment of God? Or do you despise the riches of His goodness, forbearance, and longsuffering, not knowing that **the goodness of God leads you to repentance?***

The Lord once reminded me of the pearl, created by the oyster who puts a beautiful covering around an irritating piece of sand. He said that if I would "cover" the irritations being hurled my way with love and patience and forgiveness, I would be storing up pearls in heaven! What power there is in forgiveness to pull down the barrier of sin and open eyes to God's truth, bringing light to the person in darkness!

While we are in the battle we need to remember that soldiers on the battlefield are less concerned with the wounds they receive along the way than the goal of destroying the enemy!

POWER FROM ON HIGH RELEASED TO BELIEVERS

Even before the crucifixion and resurrection Jesus had given some measure of Holy Spirit power to His followers to cast out demons, heal the sick, and preach of the kingdom of God. He told them in John 14:12,

> *Most assuredly, I say unto you, he who believes in Me, the works I do he will do also; and greater works than these he will do because I go to My Father.*

When Jesus was seen again after His death and resurrection, He spoke of an exciting **new** power that was going to come to believers! In Luke 24: 45-49 He says,

> *Thus it is written, and thus it was necessary for the Christ to suffer and to rise from the dead the third day, and that repentance and remission of sins should be preached in His name to all nations, beginning with Jerusalem. And you are witnesses of these things. Behold, I send the Promise of My Father upon you; but tarry in the city of Jerusalem until you are endued with power from on high.*

> *But you shall receive power when the Holy Spirit has come upon you; and you shall be witnesses to Me in Jerusalem, and in all Judea and Samaria, and to the end of the earth.*
> *Acts 1:8*

Then Jesus said to them again,

> *Peace to you! As the Father has sent Me, I also send you.*

And when He had said this, He breathed on them and said to them,

> *Receive the Holy Spirit. If you forgive the sins of any, they are forgiven them; if you retain the sins of any, they are retained.*
> *John 20:21-23*

Who retains sins if they are not forgiven? The person who refuses to forgive! This is a serious wake-up call to those of us with the Holy Spirit who have a judgment problem and find ourselves criticizing others!

Do you remember the story of Saul on the Damascus Road? Jesus changed Saul's name to Paul the Apostle and commissioned him for the Lord's work with the Gentiles....

> To open their eyes and to turn them from **darkness to light** and **from the power of satan to God**, that they may receive **forgiveness of sins** and an **inheritance** among those who are sanctified by faith in Me. Acts 26:17-18

Now, you might be saying, "Well... those scriptures are for those people back then in the early church." Of course they were, but once the Holy Spirit came in power upon the earth, we as believers became "a royal priesthood, a holy nation." Under the old covenant (Old Testament) the anointed priests were given the authority of God to offer the sacrificial blood of animals as an atonement for the sin of the people. Under the new covenant, **all of us that believe in Jesus Christ have been give the authority and anointing of priests to offer the sacrificial blood of Christ for the remission of the sins of those around us.** Revelation 1:5-6 says,

To Him who loved us and washed us from our sins in His own blood, and has made us kings and priests to His God and Father, to Him be glory and dominion forever and ever.

The Old Testament prophesies written below once pointed to John the Baptist and to the Messiah. But now, by the power of the Holy Spirit in your heart, these scriptures are for **YOU**, that you might walk in forgiveness to change a dark world and bring the kingdom of God to earth.

*I, the Lord have called **YOU** in righteousness and will hold **YOUR** hand; I will keep **YOU** and give **YOU** as a covenant to the Gentiles, to open blind eyes, to bring out the prisoners from the prison house. Isaiah 42: 6-7 (emphasis mine)*

Behold, I send My messenger, and he will prepare the way for Me. And the Lord, whom you seek, will suddenly come to His temple. Malachi 3:1

For me, these scriptures opened new understanding about my role as a believer. I am a KING and a PRIEST with authority to offer the sacrificial blood of Christ to remit the sin of my husband and for others! Because I am washed in the blood, I can wash others in the blood also! If I have overcome satan in my life by the blood of the Lamb, then I can use the blood of the Lamb to help others overcome satan as well!

CHAPTER 5
THE BLOOD OF THE LAMB

*And they overcame him [satan] by the blood of
the Lamb, and by the word of their testimony,
and they did not love their lives to the death.
Revelation 12:11*

Satan is called "the accuser of the brethren". But the
truth is, satan has no legal right to accuse us of our sin
when we are forgiven and our sin has been totally
destroyed by the precious blood of Jesus. Of course, he
continues to try to deceive us into believing that we
are not forgiven, because he knows that when the
barrier of sin is gone, we receive supernatural
guidance and strategy to destroy satan's works! This
truth was being proven in my own life and I confessed
and repented of the self-righteous judgment I had
spewed on my husband. While I was praying for his
salvation, I had actually held him prisoner from God's
blessings by keeping him in a cage of condemnation.
Now that **I** was forgiven, new understanding of
spiritual principles revealed a plan to help my
husband escape from his darkness.

A question came to my mind. I knew I could forgive
my husband for things he had done to hurt me, but
did I have the spiritual authority to forgive him of
other sins that had nothing to do with me? He was
basically a good person, but if the definition of sin is

"missing the mark" of God's perfect plan, there might be many other sins piling up in a day that would be a barrier to God's blessing. Jesus forgave **all** sin. It is the Father's perfect will to forgive whenever we ask by the power of the Holy Spirit. It is actually the Spirit within us that does the forgiving for we have no power on our own. But wherever we suspect that sin may be operating, it is our assignment to forgive. The Pharisees were very indignant that Jesus would think He had the authority to forgive sins, but that is because they did not recognize the power of the Holy Spirit **in** Jesus. I asked a well-known pastor this question: If, by the power of the Holy Spirit within us, we have the authority to forgive sin, why is this not preached from the pulpit? His answer was that the whole concept could be greatly misunderstood by Christians who develop a "Messiah complex" and go about in a grandiose and prideful manner, speaking forgiveness out of their flesh and not by the guidance of the Holy Spirit. I understand this, and pray that we will use this strategy in humility and submissiveness to the Spirit's leading.

Now a simple prayer was forming in my mind to pray for my husband.

> *Lord, I forgive him for the way he hurt me, and I ask You to forgive him for all his other sins. Wipe his slate clean, and bring him Your light of revelation. In Jesus' name, amen.*

In my quiet time with the Lord, He revealed to me one more direction. "**Wash** him in forgiveness, over and over. As often as I bring him to your mind during the day, wash him in forgiveness. Say that same prayer, again and again until you see the breakthrough." And so I did, repeating the essence of the prayer above, many times a day. I did not say it ritually, but sincerely from the heart, knowing that if sins were multiplying unknowingly in my husband's day, I was continually pulling the barrier down so that God's revelation could sink into his heart.

John 13 tells the story of Jesus washing the feet of His disciples. In verse 7 He says,

> *What I am doing you do not understand now, but you will know after this.*

I believe He was "washing the dirt" off the disciples in a ceremony that was symbolic to the washing of sin that would occur in a very short time at the cross. He was washing them in forgiveness by the power of the Holy Spirit. Jesus went on to say,

> *If I do not wash you, you have no part of Me.*

Speaking of the washing in His blood, He knew that they would not become part of the body of Christ until they received remission of their sins. He then commissioned them to do the same with each other in verses 14 and 15.

If I then, your Lord and Teacher, have washed your feet, you also should wash one another's feet. For I have given you an example, that you should do as I have done for you.

Actually, feet were not the issue. Jesus was saying that as He was washing them in forgiveness by the power of His blood, we should also **wash each other in forgiveness by the power of his blood.**

Don't wait to read the rest of this book....begin now! Start to wash the "unlovely" people in your life in the blood of Jesus. Not just once, but over and over, as often as the Lord brings them to mind. If you have ever cared for a toddler, you know that little people get dirty in spite of themselves, and don't know or care about needing a bath. But you, as a parent, are called to bathe their hands and faces often to protect them from disease. You don't ask yourself if you "feel" like doing it; you simply know that it's necessary or there may be worse problems down the road. So you clean them because you love them with an unconditional agape love that wants the very best for them. The "unlovely" person in your mind right now is caked with spiritual "dirt". Why don't you take a moment to pray this prayer?

Lord, I make the choice right now to take my judgment off this person. This is a hard sacrifice, because sometimes I would rather continue in anger and self-pity. I choose to forgive this person for all the hurt he has caused me. I release him to You for your perfect judgment. I know that I cannot change this person or tell him how to live his life, and I ask You to remind me regularly to release my judgments so that You can do Your work. I pray the blood of Jesus over him and I forgive him. Wipe his slate clean, Lord, and bring him Your revelation and blessing. In Jesus' name, amen.

Results
of
Forgiveness

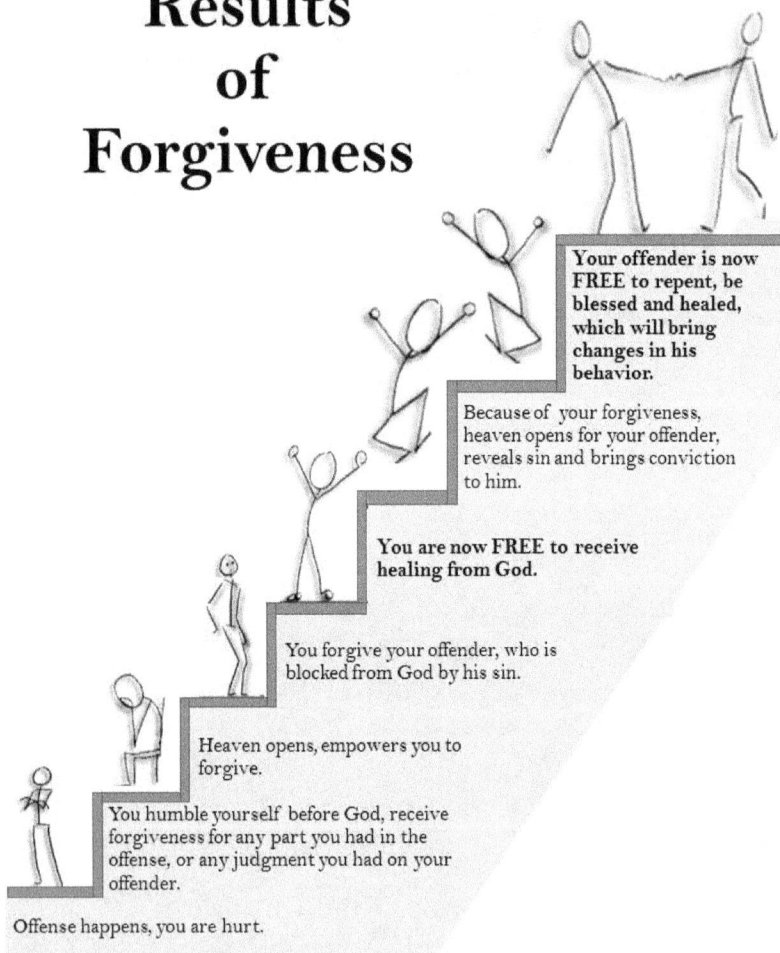

Your offender is now FREE to repent, be blessed and healed, which will bring changes in his behavior.

Because of your forgiveness, heaven opens for your offender, reveals sin and brings conviction to him.

You are now FREE to receive healing from God.

You forgive your offender, who is blocked from God by his sin.

Heaven opens, empowers you to forgive.

You humble yourself before God, receive forgiveness for any part you had in the offense, or any judgment you had on your offender.

Offense happens, you are hurt.

CHAPTER 6
THE WORD OF THE TESTIMONY

With great anticipation I began the new strategy, feeling somewhat pregnant with the Lord's promise! Over the next three months the only changes I saw were in myself. Because I was no longer allowing myself to judge, I had no desire to push Christianity in a manipulative fashion. I was no longer showing disapproval of unspiritual things, and genuine love was flowing through me. When I saw victory in prayer I would relate to my husband what the Lord had done in a very short, simple manner, and did not react to anything negative that he had to say. I was walking in peace.

Something was happening in him. He was becoming more withdrawn and depressed! One morning he sat in his chair frowning dismally. I asked if I could pray for him, and to my surprise he said yes! So I just laid my hands on his head and asked the Lord to give him peace. It was a short and quiet prayer, and he made no comment, but seemed to regain strength and went out to work in the yard.

Three weeks later we had an interesting conversation. He had been wanting to get a sports car, specifically a Porsche. He announced excitedly that he had found the right one in the paper, and that the money was coming in for it during the week. I was not all that enamored with the idea of a sports car, but I commented that "God has always been good to give us our heart's desires, hasn't He?"

He chuckled. "Yeah. I'll bet God wants to experience the Porsche through me!"

I was speechless! That's why I know that the next thing that came out of my mouth was not from me! It didn't even pass through my brain….my mouth just opened, and out it came…. **"How can He experience it through you if He isn't in you?"** I was totally shocked at what I had said, and expected a severe rebuke in return, but my husband just looked puzzled.

He asked, "What do you mean, not **in** me?

"Well, have you ever **invited** the Lord to live **in** you?" I asked in a gentler tone.

"I thought you prayed that **for** me that day you prayed. Am I supposed to do it myself? What do I have to say to invite Him in?" And he urged me to lead him the sinner's prayer right then. I was amazed! After all these years, it seemed so easy! Shouldn't we have a small orchestra or a marching band? So easy. Maybe too easy. Maybe just the first step.

SOMETHING MISSING

Up to this point I had been attending a small denominational church, but now my husband was wanting to go with me to a large non-denominational one. The very first Sunday he remarked that he had never wanted to go to church before, because the sermons seemed boring and he couldn't understand what they were talking about. At that service, everything the pastor said was perfectly clear. He also said that during praise and worship "it felt like electricity in the air". The Spirit of God was definitely at work! Time to move to the next step. So at breakfast one morning I said, "Um, ah, there's something I hadn't told you that is important when you become a Christian...."

He replied, "I know. I have to be water baptized."

Amazed, I asked, "How did you know?"

"Well, every time we go to church and I open my bulletin, the first thing I see on the page is WATER BAPTISM. Every week I see it! I guess I'll have to get water baptized!"

God was always one step ahead of me! So my husband got baptized. But there was still something missing and God revealed that even though he had accepted Christ in his heart, there was no real repentance. He is a good man, I thought. And because he did not participate in the really "bad" sins according to the world's standard, he did not see himself as a sinful person. His own sinfulness had not yet been revealed.

Then the Lord began to deal with **me**!

> *Didn't we have a plan, you and I? You were going to wash him in forgiveness, and I was going to take the blinders off his eyes. Why did you stop?*

Apparently, at the time he said the sinner's prayer I came to the conclusion that he was "IN" the kingdom of God and that I didn't need to wash him in forgiveness any longer! But he did not yet know the principles of kingdom life. It would take some time before he would understand the importance of asking the Lord to clean his heart daily. It was still my responsibility to do the washing, until he was mature enough in the faith to assume it for himself. I remembered the story of Job, who offered sacrifices daily for his grown children because he was not sure they would do it for themselves.

PRESSING THROUGH THE DARKNESS

So I began again. Now Mike was debating a career change and moving our family from Texas to Ohio, which would mean a great lifestyle change for all of us. I could see that if I resisted the move he would always wonder if he had missed the job of a lifetime. I prayed and did not see the door closing. We put the house on the market and it sold immediately. I set my mind to submit to God's will. Mom, Dad, teenage son, two birds and a dog said good-bye to warm, sunny Texas.

It began to snow as we drove into Ohio. For three months it snowed every single day. It was -27 degrees. The ground was so frozen that the dog couldn't stand on all four feet long enough to do her business! Our son experienced great difficulties with the cultural changes and school. My husband encountered a business environment totally focused on materialism. Ethics and morality suddenly became very important. He began to see how his standards compared with those who were climbing upward in wealth and power. His job involved foreign and domestic travel, so he was away often. There were two rays of "Sonshine" that year... I was blessed to find a lovely group of praying women, and our family was involved in a good solid Bible-believing church.

In the meantime, the Lord had begun to focus my husband's thinking. He realized that his work would never be fruitful as long as his value system and vision were different from the authorities in his work environment. Contacting his previous employer in Texas, he was assured of reemployment if he returned home. He finished up his last trip. Our bags were packed and we were on our way back to Texas! He hardly noticed that his leg had a peculiar ache. Probably pulled a muscle, he thought.

As we drove south toward Houston, the leg was becoming very painful. Now he was having trouble breathing, and breaking into cold sweats. I felt an urgency from the Lord to get him to the hospital quickly.

The diagnosis: a life-threatening blood clot, with multiple pulmonary emboli. He was sent immediately to ICU. The grace of God somehow rested like a cocoon around me as I prayed for the Lord to use this circumstance for His own divine purposes. I washed him in forgiveness all the more, because I knew that keeping the barrier of sin away from him would be crucial to his healing. When my husband relates this story now, he says he knew from the start that in spite of bad reports and worried looks from the medical staff around him, he would be fine! Absolute peace guarded his heart that whole week. When he was released from the hospital we finished the moving process, settling into a temporary rental house. His physical condition, however, had been seriously weakened by the illness and the move. In retrospect, I now see that God was just waiting for the perfect time when, in my husband's weakness, He would show Himself strong.

BREAKING THROUGH

One morning I awoke to find my husband sitting in the living room distraught and guilt-ridden, emotional and tearful, which was totally unlike his usual strong, self-assured demeanor. He said he had a dream in which he saw situations throughout his life in which he had made poor decisions, hurt people, and had bad attitudes. In the dream, his life had literally been laid out before him like a video, and he saw all the things he had done wrong. He was gripped with conviction. In Ohio his moral standards were looking good compared to the materialistic environment around him. But now his standards were being compared with the holiness of God, and God's light was shining into the darkness of his heart. The Lord put His words into my mouth.

> *Could you ever pay the price for all these things you have done? You don't have to! Someone already paid it for you. Now you can understand why Jesus paid such a price on the cross, and all that is left for you to do is to ask His forgiveness. Do you want to?*

Of course, he did, gratefully accepting God's precious gift, and also asking Jesus again to come and live in his heart.

He was very tired, so I left him in the chair sleeping and went out to do some errands. I was still in awe about the events of the morning. And what a strange morning it was....the rain had cleared and a beautiful, full color, complete rainbow filled the sky. The still, small voice in my heart said, *The promise has come to pass.* There was a knowing in me that something spectacular had happened, but I didn't have complete understanding of what that was, or what "the promise" meant.

When I returned home, my husband told an amazing story. Asleep in his chair, he heard a knock at the door. In his dream he went and opened the door, to find the Lord standing there in incredibly brilliant light. Jesus entered the doorway with His arms open and extended, drawing my husband into the brightness, enveloping him in love and comfort. At this point, he woke up. Believing that someone was really knocking at the door, he went to see. Finding no one there, he returned to his chair, fell off to sleep again, and the dream resumed exactly where it had been interrupted. Jesus sat down on the sofa. My husband puzzled, "*I don't understand this part, but I became a little boy again, and I crawled up into His lap. He didn't speak. He just comforted me and loved me.*"

Because my husband was not acquainted with the Word of God, he did not know these scriptures at the time:

> *Behold, I stand at the door and knock. If any man hear My voice and open the door, I will*

come in to him and dine with him, and he with Me. Revelation 3:20

Let the little children come unto Me, and do not forbid them, for of such is the kingdom of God. Assuredly, I say unto you, whoever does not receive the kingdom of God as a little child will by no means enter it. And he took them up in His arms, put His hands on them, and blessed them. Mark 10:14-16

There are no words that can adequately describe the love of our Savior. I could have told my husband all about Jesus, and bored him in the telling, for he would not have understood. But God had a better plan. That day my husband **met** Jesus. In the light and comfort and love of a Jesus hug, many wounds from my husband's childhood were healed. Peace came into our home that day. Charles Wesley, in his classic hymn *Love Divine, All Loves Excelling*, seems to have known the ecstasy of the soul that is touched by the tenderness of the Lord the way my husband was touched that morning.

Love divine, all loves excelling
Joy of heaven to earth come down.
Fix in us Thy humble dwelling,
All Thy faithful mercies crown,
Jesus, Thou art all compassion,
Pure, unbounded love Thou art,
Visit us with Thy salvation,
Enter every trembling heart.

CHAPTER 7

WE LOVE NOT OUR LIVES UNTO DEATH

I have become very militant about defeating the devil and his works in my life! I am not content with occasional victories anymore. I know that in God's plan, according to Revelation 12:11, we are well able to overcome satan on a regular basis. Let's look at that scripture again.

> *And they overcame him [satan] by the blood of the Lamb and by the word of their testimony, and they did not love their lives to the death.*

We have seen in the last two chapters how the blood of Jesus cleanses us from all iniquity to remove the barrier that hides us from God's presence. Therefore, by confession, repentance, and forgiveness of others, we are able to receive TRUTH from God, which cancels all deceptions and lies of satan. We heard the word of the testimony, that praying the blood of Jesus and forgiving others opens heaven so that we all can have fellowship with Him.

When we receive the word of God and become "doers" of the word, we are applying God's principles to fight the darkness of satan. The strategies that He teaches us **always work**, when we are consistent and persistent and use them in faith. Therefore, if we have

---

been obedient to do what He has told us, we will soon have a testimony of God's faithfulness! That will build our faith to believe in God's word for the next battle, and will build up the strength of other believers who are fighting the same battles. They, too, will defeat the enemy because of the word of the testimony.

The third section of this scripture is a part that is often ignored when the scripture is quoted. Yet, in some ways, it is the most important concept of all. We do not like talking about *dying*, but dying to the ego within us, the self-focus and independence, and self-protective devices, is a necessary part of becoming Christlike and having the authority and anointing of Jesus to defeat satan.

Long ago, before this story began, I **knew** that my way of life was hindering me from God's best. Addiction, selfish decisions and the inability to love unconditionally were fueling strife in my family and interrupting the work of the Lord. I tried to change, but could not do it myself. Like the Apostle Paul, I wondered why I continually did the things I didn't want to do, and didn't do the things I should do! Just being honest with God I said, *"How do I die to self? If You will teach me how to do this, I will gladly die. But I don't know how!"*

THE RIVER OF LIFE

A picture emerged in my mind of a mighty river beginning to flow from the throne of God. My soul at that time was a series of stagnant puddles, muddy with old thinking patterns, wrong perceptions, half-truths, and bondages of fear and uncertainty. I had many doubts about my own capabilities and doubts about God's love for me. I knew that God **could** do anything, but I was not sure that He loved me enough to **want** to. The mighty river of God's life began to flow into my heart after I prayed that prayer about dying to self. I began to let go of the old and receive the new, as God began to bring people into my life that could disciple me in the ways of the Lord.

I know now that without the renewal of my mind I would not have been able to "stand" in faith through this process of unconditional love and forgiveness. I began using my new strategy both at home and, as the Holy Spirit led me, in other places. I began sharing this plan with other believers who were struggling as I was. I found that some people can take this good news, run with it, and achieve results quickly. Here is just a small sample of the many testimonies that we celebrated:

- A mother praying forgiveness over her son saw him take the ungodly books he'd been reading to the back yard and burn them, then recommit his life to Christ.

- An anointed intercessor prayed for two pastors in a community who were offended with one another and would not join a local pastor's coalition. After a short time of "washing" them in forgiveness, they were reconciled and joined the group.

- A teacher's prejudicial attitude toward a child completely changed when the mother "washed" the teacher daily in forgiveness.

- A businesswoman relaxed her control and agreed to compromise in a business deal when she was washed in forgiveness by those who were being dealt with unfairly.

- A jail inmate received time and attention from her previously neglectful court-appointed lawyer when she "washed" him daily in forgiveness.

- Many marriages have been saved when one spouse prayed forgiveness faithfully over the other.

I found that those who were successful with standing in daily forgiveness were the ones who had previously received some emotional healing from the Lord and were committed to "dying to self", becoming Christ-like, and having victory over satan.

Those who were **not** successful were the ones who gave up easily, and were not consistent or persistent.

But I am not judging them because there was a good reason for this! People who are emotionally wounded from their past live with pain in their souls. Do you remember that we briefly discussed the *backlash* that comes when the person we are praying for begins to receive conviction from God about their sin? That person may get very irritable until the final breakthrough, and the intercessor must have "standing power" to hang in there. If intercessors are carrying unhealed emotional pain from the past, the additional pain from that backlash will overwhelm them and cause them to give up the process.

My son presented me with an awesome example of the power of unconditional love overcoming the need for self-protection. My husband had designed a beautifully landscaped garden on our back yard. A feral cat sought out a cozy place under a bush and gave birth to three kittens, two female and one male. By the time their eyes had opened and they were moving around, the mom had disappeared. We brought them into our bathroom so that we could acclimate them to people and eventually adopt them out. The two little ladies bonded to us immediately, purred and loved to be held. But the male was a spit-fire! Whenever we entered the bathroom he would run behind a plant, hissing and striking out with his claws. There was no way I was getting near that cat! It was sad, though, because if the cat was not adoptable, he would at some point have to be put down. But one day my son went into that room and came out with the little spit-fire plastered to his chest and he was forcibly and furiously petting that cat! I said, "*What are you doing?*"

He replied, "*Well, the cat needed love, so I decided to give him some!*"

Amazed, I asked, "*Weren't you afraid he would bite and claw you?*"

"*Naw,*" my son replied. "*Scratches and bites will heal. But this guy needed love even though he didn't know it, and that was more important.*"

He held and petted that cat for hours, and by the end of the day it had succumbed to the power of love and had become sweet, trusting, and adoptable. My son had "standing power". Backlash did not affect him. We need that same endurance with the unlovely people around us. Let's look at the things that keep us from operating in that unconditional love.

When we are hurt, the situation is retained in memory... the look on the offender's face, the body language, the tone of voice, and other reminders of what wounded us. So when we run into a similar situation later in life, such as someone giving us the same look, or using the same tone of voice, or having the same attitude as the original offender, that wounded place within us becomes an emotional "trigger button". Without even thinking, we react with anger or resentment or fear or downright retaliation, protecting ourselves from more pain. However, in doing so, we end up hurting the one who is hurting us! And that person will now hurt us more out of his own desire for self-protection. And so the damage in both parties escalates, and the sin on both sides keeps us separated from God. So if, for instance, a wife is praying forgiveness over her husband and he begins to get conviction but does not like what he is feeling, his own trigger buttons will send him into "backlash". If her emotional pain from the past has been healed, she will recognize this as a **good sign**, not taking it personally. She will press in even harder in forgiveness until the breakthrough! But if she is not healed, and there are still trigger buttons within her, when the backlash comes, she will feel wounded. She will react with negative emotion, making the situation worse, and bringing the forgiveness strategy to a halt. She will need inner healing before she starts up again!

Let me give you a personal example. Before the Lord revealed the forgiveness strategy to me, the misery that I had felt in my marriage had a lot to do with wounds that I had from my family of origin. Now, lest you think I am "krino-judging", let me explain! Children are very poor interpreters of the situations they find themselves in. So I believed things that were fabricated out of my childish interpretations, such as:

I am not loved; I am all alone.
I have to do everything the way others want me
to do it, or I will not be approved or loved.
If something goes wrong, it is my fault.
I don't measure up to everybody else.

My parents were not necessarily at fault, they were just human and had trigger buttons of their own. So my memory retained the look and tone of voice my father had when he was angry. And the condescending manner of my mother when I didn't meet her standards. Both of them acted out of their childish interpretations of what *their* parents did! And so every generation was somehow wounded from the generation before it, all the way back to Adam and Eve! But when I got married, I carried the trigger buttons from my past into the marriage, and my husband did the same thing. We reacted to each other's manner, and tone of voice, and body language. We wounded each other more and more. If he said something in the same way my father would have said it when he was annoyed, the little girl in me would stamp her foot and retaliate in angry, resentful thoughts. If I suggested something that needed to be done, the little boy in him would react to the orders and directions of his mother, and he would isolate and go silent, which only triggered me more, because I was ready to spew my bitterness into the air! And until my pain was so intense that I finally humbled myself before the Lord, our marriage was doomed.

Thank God Who revealed Himself to me and then to my husband, and brought us healing and wholeness. Of course, the plan of satan was to steal, kill and destroy this marriage. God's plan was to train us to be warriors in the army of God, save the marriage, and pass the strategy of forgiveness on to save many more.

I realize now that God prepared me for the battle in three ways: He exposed the lies of the enemy that I had believed and filled me with the truth of His word, and He connected me with a person that led me through the process of emotional healing.

I learned this interesting fact:

AS MY SOUL IS HEALED, THE HOLY SPIRIT HAS MORE FREEDOM TO TAKE POSSESSION OF ME. AS THE HOLY SPIRIT TAKES POSSESSION OF ME, I RECEIVE THE STRENGTH TO DIE TO SELF.

That's a pretty big mouthful, so let's break it down!

A wounded soul strongly protects itself from more pain.

It is cluttered with "rights" that it wants to hold onto. To be honest, it is self-focused and consumed with the desire to comfort self and build up the ego. We may invite the Spirit of God to dwell within us, but until we do some necessary cleaning out, there is not a lot of room for the Holy Spirit to operate. It is said that it is not how much we have the Holy Spirit that counts, but how much the Holy Spirit has us! When we were hurt in the past, often in our childhood, satan was right there to introduce some lies to us. Lies like,

There is something wrong with you.

God doesn't love you.

You are all alone.

You are a failure.

You need to pretend you are something you aren't.

You need to watch out for #1, because no one else will protect you.

God can't be trusted.

There is no God.

There is no devil.

You need to do unto others before they do unto you.

Those are just a few of the deceptions that satan introduces to us when we are in a traumatized or wounded state. His basic purpose is to keep us from ever finding out who God is, how much God loves us, who we are, and the power of God that is within us to destroy the works of the devil. He plants the lies early in life, and then reinforces them with negative situations along the way. By the time we come into adulthood, when we could be wielding the Sword of the Spirit to destroy satan's works, we have been rendered so ineffective and powerless that we don't even try. This is the goal of the enemy.

About the time I was challenging God to teach me how to die, I came across a book by Robert McGee called **Search for Significance**. In this book, four major lies of the devil were exposed, and I was shocked to find that I had believed every one of them. They are listed here:

1. **I must meet certain standards in order to feel good about myself.**

2. **I must be approved by certain others to feel good about myself.**

3. **Those who fail are unworthy of love and deserve to be punished.**

4. **I must always be what I have been and live with whatever self-worth I have. I am what I am. I cannot change. I am hopeless.**

Each of these lies are replaced by the truth written in the word of God.

The following are my interpretations of the scriptures.

1. **We are not bound to the standards of men. Romans 5:1 says that we have been justified through our faith in Jesus Christ and what**

He did for us on the cross. Therefore we can have peace with God and ourselves.

2. **We are not bound to the approval of men. Colossians 1: 21-22 says that we are reconciled to God because of what Jesus Christ did on the cross, and we have God's full approval.**

3. **We are not bound to blame and condemnation. I John 4: 9-10 says that Jesus Christ satisfied the wrath of God in paying for our sins and we do not have to condemn ourselves or anyone else.**

4. **We are not bound to what we have been in the past. II Corinthians 5:17 says that we are becoming new and more Christ-like every day.**

I have put these truths into my own words, but I suggest that you find a copy of Robert McGee's book that explains each lie and truth in much better detail. These truths began a cascade of healing events in my life. I wrote them on 3x5 cards and kept them in my purse. Whenever I felt negative or uncomfortable about a situation, I would get them out, and usually discovered that I was believing one of those four lies. Soon, I was recognizing the lies without looking at the cards, and I was doing what the Bible tells us to do,

Casting down arguments and every high thing that exalts itself against the knowledge of God, bringing every thought into captivity to the obedience of Christ.   II Corinthians 10:5

If you abide in My word, you are My disciples indeed. And you shall know the truth, and the truth shall make you free. John 8: 31-32

Discovering these lies of the enemy and replacing them with God's word had a major impact on my self-image. I did not allow people to determine my value any longer. God's opinion was the only consideration, and He alone gave significance to my life. Discovering that I was a precious child of God set me free to grow closer to the Lord without fear. I began to see myself as a person with divine purpose, created uniquely for God's special work. In anticipation of great adventure, I reported for duty in His holy army!

THE BOOT CAMP OF INNER HEALING

When a soldier joins the army, he is required to get cleaned up, have his hair shaved, get his shots, and go through many rigorous tasks to build him up physically, mentally, and emotionally. He will not be sent out to war until he is at his best, prepared to win! So I entered a stage of preparation for the holy army that was not pleasant or comfortable in any way, but a necessary part of my training.

Another way to say this is... I was learning to become the Bride of Christ. It takes cooperation and work along with the Holy Spirit to become beautiful in the soul.

Ezekiel 36:23-36 tells us that the Lord does healing of the heart in us, so that His name will ultimately be honored!

> *And I will sanctify My great name, which has been profaned among the nations, which you have profaned in their midst; and the nations shall know that I am the Lord God, when I am hallowed in you before their eyes. For I will take you from among the nations, gather you out of all countries, and bring you into your own land. Then I will sprinkle clean water on you, and you shall be clean. I will cleanse you from all filthiness and from all your idols. I will give you a new heart and put a new spirit within you. I will take the heart of stone out of your flesh, and give you a heart of flesh. I will put My Spirit within you and cause you to walk in My statutes, and you will keep My judgments and do them. Then you shall dwell in the land that I gave to your fathers. You shall be My people, and I will be your God.*

> *I will deliver you from all your uncleanness. I will call for the grain and multiply it, and bring no famine among you. And I will multiply the fruit of your trees and the increase of your fields, so that you need never*

again bear the reproach of famine among the nations... (vs. 33) Thus says the Lord God, on the day that I cleanse you from all your iniquities, I will also enable you to dwell in the cities, and the ruins shall be rebuilt. The desolate land shall be tilled instead of lying desolate in the sight of all who pass by.

So they will say, "This land that was desolate has become like the Garden of Eden, and the wasted, desolate, and ruined cities are now fortified and inhabited." Then the nations which are left all around you shall know that I, the Lord, have rebuilt the ruined places and planted what was desolate. I, the Lord, have spoken it, and I will do it.

Yes! That is exactly what He did! He led me to a compassionate, Spirit-filled intercessor-counselor who helped me through this process. As the Lord brought up painful memories in my mind, she helped me to:

- Receive forgiveness
- Forgive myself
- Forgive each and every person who had hurt me
- Break generational iniquities that had come down my family bloodline
- Dissolve soul ties

- Break the power of the occult
- Bind and oust demonic spirits
- And ask Jesus to come into every wounded place, touch, and heal

This was all done in a five hour period. Everything changed that day! Twenty years of various addictive behaviors were totally broken! The anger inside that had caused me to speak jokes with "double meanings" and make critical remarks that brought embarrassment and shame upon the members of my family had disappeared! And in the place of the constant chaotic rushing in my soul, there was a quietness I had never known before. I had thought that I knew what the word *peace* meant, but truly I had never experienced peace before in my life. I had "died" to the fear and shame and pain in my soul that had kept me on a continual treadmill, trying to win acceptance and approval, always feeling inadequate, always working harder but never accomplishing enough. It was a darkness that I could not overcome on my own. But forgiveness was what ushered in the light, and healing began.

What other things have changed because of this healing? My prayers are heard and answered! Always! And physically, I am much healthier. I accomplish more tasks with greater value in shorter time as I am open to hearing direction from the Lord. My relationships are more meaningful. My creativity is expanding daily, as the Lord puts His creativity in me! In fact, where life was such a burden before, now I am having fun! I look forward to every day, not knowing what exciting God encounters I may have. With Jesus, every day is an adventure! Our God is so incredibly loving and powerful in cleansing a heart!

Since that day, I have pursued the subject of inner healing and received training in many different methods, and have done inner healing with others for more than 20 years. We always begin with forgiveness. Since that is your starting point, I recommend again that you go to the **Appendix** section at the end of this book and do a thorough "cleaning out" by saying the **Forgiveness Prayers.** You will find heaven open to you, and feel a tremendous sense of relief when you have completely forgiven all who have caused you pain in your life. Begin right now!

Since this book is focused on the process of forgiveness, I will not elaborate more on the rest of the inner healing process. But instead, I refer you to a book that I wrote on that subject called, **Would You Believe? A Personal Guide to Inner Healing** which explains in more detail a way that you can meet God by yourself and work through your inner healing with Him without necessarily finding an intercessor-counselor right away. A Kindle version can be found on Amazon, and paper copies can be ordered using the e-mail address in the back of this book.

BEARING FRUIT

If you were to buy and plant a high quality fruit tree, only to discover after you had planted it that it was infested with bugs, what would you do? You would find a bug spray that would overcome those nasty critters, and cleanse the tree. Without the hindrances caused by bugs, the tree could grow healthy and strong, and one day produce beautiful fruit. This is the aim of the Lord with us, that as He cleanses us with His potent life-giving blood, we will begin producing the fruits of the Spirit listed in Galatians 5:22-25:

> But the fruit of the Spirit is love, joy, peace, longsuffering, kindness, goodness, faithfulness, gentleness, self-control. Against such there is no law. And those who are Christ's have crucified the flesh with its passions and desires. If we live in the Spirit, let us also walk in the Spirit.

The fruits of the Spirit are a magnet to those who need a touch from God. A person walking in the Spirit has a glow, a humility and gentleness that supernaturally draws others into the presence of God. Jesus drew the multitudes, the sheep without a shepherd, so that God could love them, teach them, and heal them. The Spirit has been imparted to us for the same reason, that by being Christlike, we can make an impact on the earth and bring honor to the name of the Lord.

One big area of our lives that requires us to "die to self" is in the area of holding onto our rights. Jesus was not a "self-serving" person. He and the Father were One. In John 14:12, Jesus tells us that we will *do greater works* than He did. But that is only true if we are walking in the Spirit as One with the Father like Jesus. That means giving up our self-serving attitudes and, in many cases, our rights. Under the direction of God the Father, Jesus gave up all of His rights, died for us, bought us back from satan, took the keys of hell, and was given all authority to overcome principalities and powers in the spirit realm.

When you have been liberated from the lies that satan has planted in you, and when light is flooding your heart, you will know the truth, that God is with you, protecting you, helping you, guiding you in every situation. You will have peace. You will not have to defend yourself or hold onto your "rights". You will no longer be "triggered" emotionally into ungodly behavior. Peace is the foundation for authority. When you pray in authority, God hears and answers, and the demonic get out of the way!

Cindy Jacobs, in her book called **Possessing the Gates of the Enemy,** spoke of the rights that we would have to give up in order to pull down strongholds. Strongholds are fortresses in the soul that have been built by lies and deceptions of satan, and have become a home for demonic spirits. My alcohol addiction was a stronghold. The sweet lady who did inner healing with me gave up her right that day to go shopping, or visit friends, or whatever she might do to have a nice day. Her sacrifice, her "fruit", and the power of God within her brought light to me, and the stronghold was broken. Giving up our rights to do what God wants is another part of dying to self. And as we "die", **resurrection power,** the **dunamis** dynamic power of God flows through us and around us to those who are near. Here is what Cindy says:

> *Any right that we try to hold onto will be played upon by the enemy of our souls in time of battle. Some of the rights we have to give up in order to tear down strongholds are:*
>
> *The right to be offended*
>
> *The right to our time*
>
> *The right to do what we want with our possessions*
>
> *The right to self-pity*
>
> *The right to self-justification*
>
> *The right to be understood*
>
> *The right to criticize*

We each have certain rights that matter more to us than others. I don't have a hard time giving up possessions, but I have held on to my right to be understood like a bulldog! And self-pity has been a ruthless enemy to my soul. Oswald Chambers says,

> *No sin is worse than the sin of self-pity, because it obliterates God and puts self-interest on the throne.*

Ouch! I get it! It is virtually impossible to wallow in self-pity or nurture an offence while forgiving someone who has hurt you. You will have to choose one or the other, your way or God's.

BROKENNESS IS GOOD

When we are hurt by others, especially the ones we love the most, we feel like our hearts are breaking. Many other kinds of loss in our lives also make us feel "broken" inside. Loss of a job, loss of relationships, loss of money, a home, health. So many situations in this fallen world bring brokenness. But brokenness of the soul is a necessary part of the "dying to self" process. If we embrace brokenness under the Lord's direction, it will also break the self-centered soul within.

Watchman Nee speaks of this in his book **The Release of the Spirit.** He compares the soul with the alabaster box that Mary broke to release the precious perfume poured over Jesus. Likewise, we are earthen vessels that must be broken, in order to release the power of the Spirit from within. Here is his description:

> *Our spirit is released according to the degree of our brokenness. The one who has accepted the most discipline is the one who can best serve. The more one is broken, the more sensitive he is. The more loss one has suffered, the more he has to give. Wherever we desire to save ourselves, in that thing we become spiritually useless. Whenever we preserve and excuse ourselves, at that point we are deprived of spiritual sensitivity and supply. Let no one imagine he can be effective and disregard this basic principle.*

Those who hurt you are those who are hurt themselves.

Hurting people hurt people.

Every crisis and loss in your life is an opportunity for God to show you His love, work in your soul, and touch the souls of others for Him.

Through forgiveness and inner healing, you can come to a place of peace and bring God's healing to those who have hurt you. All it takes is submission to the transformational power of God. Let me pose a question to you that Oswald Chambers has asked:

Are we willing to surrender our grasp on all that we possess, our desires, and everything else in our lives? Are we ready to be identified with the death of Jesus Christ? Make a determination to go on through the crisis, surrendering all that you have and all that you are to Him. And God will then equip you to do all that He requires of You.

I SURRENDER ALL

My husband owns a female macaw named Pheenie. This is a large tropical bird with a tremendously powerful beak. The bird loves him, but is very jealous of me, so I keep my distance! One day my husband inadvertently left the cage door partially open and went off to work. When I heard strange noises coming from that room and went to check, there was the macaw, proudly perched on top of her cage, eating my silk flower arrangement! It would not be simple to get my husband back home because work was an hour away and he was still in route.

I called a friend to pray, then got a broom and stepped up to the cage. The bird looked down on me from her high position, believing that she was much bigger than I, and was quite in charge. She opened her beak and spread her wings in a threatening manner, as if to say, *"One step closer and I will eat you for breakfast."* I retreated and prayed again. She began to pridefully strut back and forth, hungrily eyeing the furniture that she would demolish next. I raised the broom and began to prod her gently in the direction I wished her to go. She fought the broom, but eventually got tired and flopped down on the floor. Now she looked wistfully at her cage, wanting the comfort and security of home. But the door was far enough from the floor that she would need help getting in, since she was not a flier. I laid down the broom and moved closer. This time, she looked up at my face and crouched in submission. How had I managed to get so big? Her pride was gone. She was in a helpless situation. I put my arm under her breast and gave the order that my husband gives, "STEP UP." She stepped up onto my arm, and I carried her where I wanted her to go... back into her cage.

The Lord began to speak to me about how much I was like that bird. Only when we see how little we are and how big God is do we finally give up our own strength and pride and independence, and STEP UP on the Lord's mighty right arm so that He can take us where He wants us to go, in His strength!

> *Humble yourself in the sight of the Lord, and He will lift you up. James 4:10*

Oh, Lord, prod me until I surrender all. One day I will stand before your throne and all that I did in my own strength will burn up like wood, hay and stubble. But what I did while riding submissively on Your right arm will be gold, stored up for me in heaven. Purify my heart, Lord, so that I can bring honor to Your name!

CHAPTER 8
CONFORMING TO THE PATTERN

Patterns, molds, and stencils are very helpful tools in life. The Lord has given us creativity so that we can be free, but without boundaries and discipline we can easily go far afield and "miss the mark" of God's plan for us.

Suppose I am making a shirt. I will lay out the material that I am going to use, but then I will lay the pattern on top of the material, pin it down solidly, and carefully cut away every bit of cloth that does not conform to the pattern. Then I can guarantee to have a shirt of the right form and size.

God's pattern for your life is His Word. We already read the passage about *"taking every thought captive and bringing it to the obedience of Christ".* Surrendering to God means accepting the pattern of God's direction and conforming our thoughts to God's thoughts, instead of continually doing things our own way.

Our natural inclination is to follow the pattern that was set before us by our own families. If our own parents were critical and judgmental, easily offended, and believed there was honor in taking action to self-protect or to change the behaviors of others, then that is what "seems right" to us, and we follow their pattern. But God's pattern is totally different. He brings about change with the power of love, and it is purely supernatural! Jesus was one with His Father, and followed His Father's direction in everything. When He did take action, throwing the money changers' tables out of the temple, He did it under the direction of the Father. When He was falsely accused, convicted and tortured, He said not a word. It was the Father's plan. If the Father held the pattern on Jesus, and we have allowed Jesus to hold the pattern on us, then our children are very fortunate, because it will then be natural for them to stay within the boundaries of love that God has provided. However, because many of us had not surrendered to that pattern when we were raising our children, rebellion has made its way down the family line. Not to worry! We have been forgiven, and as we forgive our children, they too, will receive the love of God and begin to want the things God wants for their lives. Our blessing comes as we nestle into God's loving hand, receiving His warmth, His nurturing, His goodness, His protection and peace, and then passing that on to others! The Presence of the Living God in you will bring changes to the people around you in ways you cannot imagine!

But let's go back to what seems to come easiest to us. When others hurt us, our natural tendency is to fight them and punish them, either physically or mentally, for our own self-protection. When we *"die to self"* we put ourselves in God's hands for His protection, trusting God's love and character. We lay down our weapons. We submit ourselves just like that piece of material, to God, and He superimposes His Word upon us and gently cuts away all that does not come into agreement with His Word. Are you ready? Lay down and be still....here comes the pattern!

> *For all have sinned and come short of the glory of God. Romans 3:23*

> *If we confess our sins, He is faithful and just to forgive us our sins and to cleanse us from all unrighteousness. I John 1:9*

That was the easy part. Your sins are washed away...forever! Heaven is open to you! God loves you, and He is healing you, and all of His provision is available to you! Remember though, that you must be willing to RECEIVE forgiveness before you will be able to GIVE forgiveness to others. So make sure you have released yourself from judgement, and that you are allowing the blood sacrifice of Jesus to actually cleanse you of the unrighteousness.

> *If you forgive men their trespasses, your Heavenly Father will also forgive you. But if you do not forgive men their trespasses, neither will your Father forgive your trespasses. Matthew 6: 14-15*

Judge not, that you be not judged. For with what judgment you judge, you will be judged; And with the same measure you use, it will be measured back to you. Matthew 7:1-2

And why do you look at the speck in your brother's eye, but do not perceive the plank in your own eye? Or how can you say to your brother, "Brother, let me remove the speck that is in your eye" when you ourself do not see the plank that is in your own eye? Hypocrite! First, remove the plank from your own eye, and then you will see clearly to remove the speck that is in your brother's eye. Luke 6:41-42

Therefore you are inexcusable, O man, whoever you are who judge, for in whatever you judge another you condemn yourself; for you who judge practice the same things. Romans 2:1

Do not speak evil of one another, brethren. He who speaks evil of a brother and judges his brother, speaks evil of the law and judges the law. But if you judge the law, you are not a doer of the law, but a judge. There is one Lawgiver who is able to save and to destroy. Who are you to judge another? James 4:11-12

Well. That cut was kind of painful. Didn't I just confess my sins? I don't like to be reminded that I have *more!*

Sometimes I want justice for the people who hurt me, but mercy for myself. I want the right to "play God" and be the judge. But I forget that I am just as imperfect as those who have offended me, and that Jesus died for them, too. However....I am ready to recognize my sin and confess it and receive forgiveness and cleansing....again!

> *Then Peter came to Him and said, "Lord, how often shall my brother sin against me and forgive him? Up to seven times?" Jesus said to him, "I do not say to you up to seven times, but up to seventy times seven." Matthew 18: 21-22*

Oh, my, that is tedious! *Why would You want me to be hurt again and again, Lord?* Oh. You are saying that You will give me the grace to stand and persevere in forgiveness. That you want to change *them* but I have to keep heaven open for them so they can see their own sin and be empowered with grace to change. That you want to grow some more fruit in me in the area of *patience and kindness and goodness and faithfulness and self-control.* And that whatever woundedness I get in the battle, no matter how deep, You will heal. Ok, I can live with that. (I hear God saying, "Yes, you can really *live* with that!! And your offenders can, too!)

> *Repay no one evil for evil. Have regard for good things in the sight of all men. If it is possible, as much as depends on you, live*

peaceably with all men. Beloved, do not avenge yourselves, but rather give place to wrath; for it is written, "Vengeance is Mine, I will repay", says the Lord. Romans 12:17-19

Do not be deceived, God is not mocked; for whatever a man sows, that will he also reap. Galatians 6:7

But he who does wrong will be repaid for the wrong which he has done, and there is no partiality. Colossians 3:25

So if I forgive, and keep forgiving, I am not just letting the offender get by with what he has done?

God has made a Covenant with you to be with you always. He loves you and He loves the offender. He will do what is best for both. And your offender will be facing God as an adversary if he keeps tormenting you.

Beloved, do not avenge yourselves, but rather give place to wrath, for it is written, "Vengeance is Mine, I will repay," says the Lord. Romans 12:19

God's vengeance usually is lifting His hand of protection briefly to allow the offender to reap what he has sown and experience something similar to what he has done to others.

God is just saying, "If you are being pushed around by a bully, don't try to handle it all by yourself! Bring the bully to your Daddy God, and He will take care of the problem for you". And that takes a great deal of trust on our part. It is another area He wants us to grow in, because once we see how things change when we let God take control, the more we will put things in His hands, and the more successes we will have.

> *But I say to you, love your enemies, bless those who curse you, do good to those who hate you, and pray for those who spitefully use you and persecute you. Matthew 5:44*

> *Be kind to one another, tenderhearted, forgiving one another, just as God in Christ has forgiven you. Ephesians 4:32*

But doesn't that make me a hypocrite? I don't feel like loving them! Forgiveness is love. It is an act of your will, not your emotions. When you commit yourself to conform to the pattern that Jesus set for us in forgiveness and kindness, your emotions will eventually come in line, because that is part of the healing that takes place in you. Jesus touches the wounds in your soul and pours Himself into you so that you have His heart. And if you are suffering from physical illness, that will be healed along the way.

In doing inner healing prayer with people, I have noticed that there are various stages of forgiveness. It is never a "one time" decision, but is a process that involves daily decisions to let God change us and change our offenders.

First stage: **Agreeing** to forgive, **let go** of judgment, and **release** the person to God for His work in that person. And agreeing, when we drop the offense, to let our actions **show** that we have forgiven by being kind, gentle, good, patient ....in other words, allowing God's Spirit to grow **fruits** in us!

Second stage: Allowing God to show us why the offender is acting the way they are. In this stage, the victim must be willing to see the situation from the offender's point of view. Only God can impart this kind of knowledge. This must be done in intimate prayer time with the Lord. In this stage we learn humility and patience.

Third stage: The victim **identifies** himself with Christ. His own fleshly desires to self-protect are gone. He is filled with unconditional love for the offender. The love of God Himself flows through him. In the spirit realm, the demonic cannot remain around the offender, when God's love surrounds him. This is the love that never fails.

I truly believe that the third stage only comes as the victim is conformed to Christ in the *dunamis* power that Jesus experienced in the resurrection. It is dynamite power of the Holy Spirit to make all things new. If you genuinely want a NEW YOU, then ask the

Lord to download *dunamis* power to conform you to the pattern that Christ has modeled for you and you will be filled with love you have never experienced before.

Dr. Martin Luther King, Jr. left us with a wonderful legacy of God-given words of wisdom. Among them are these:

> *Darkness cannot drive out darkness; only light can do that. Hate cannot drive out hate; only love can do that.*

> *I have decided to stick with love. Hate is too great a burden to bear.*

> *Love is the only force capable of transforming an enemy into a friend.*

> *We must develop and maintain the capacity to forgive. He who is devoid of the power to forgive is devoid of the power to love. There is some good in the worst of us and some evil in the best of us. When we discover this, we are less prone to hate our enemies.*

> *Human progress is neither automatic nor inevitable... Every step toward the goal of justice requires sacrifice, suffering, and struggle; the tireless exertions and passionate concern of dedicated individuals.*

Every man must decide whether he will walk in the light of creative altruism or in the darkness of destructive selfishness.

Are you beginning to see that forgiveness is the vehicle through which trees of righteousness (us!) produce great fruits (fruits of the Spirit) for the healing of the world around us? Forgiveness is the love of the Father expressed through us on the earth.

I love this Message Bible version of I Corinthians 13: 4-7: (bold print is mine)

Love never gives up.

Love cares more for others than for self.

Love doesn't want what it doesn't have.

Love doesn't strut,

Doesn't have a swelled head,

Doesn't force itself on others,

Isn't always "me first",

Doesn't fly off the handle,

Doesn't keep score of the sins of others,

Doesn't revel when others grovel,

Takes pleasure in the flowering of truth,

Puts up with anything,

Trusts God always,

Always looks for the best,

Never looks back,

But keeps going to the end.

This is our pattern. Impossible? No. It is God Who is forming us, not ourselves. We surrender. We submit in trust. We are made new! We are the material that lays beneath the pattern, humbly waiting to be transformed to the image of Christ. Like a butterfly, you will never know the amazing freedom and beauty that God has for you until you shed the old thinking patterns and lies and actions that have held you prisoner in your cocoon. Let go of your fear and control! Set your heart today on living life according to God's Word, let Him take you through the process and get free!

CHAPTER 9

WALKING IT OUT: THE NUTS AND BOLTS OF FORGIVENESS

A little four year old boy was being taught The Lord's Prayer by his mother. As she said the phrases, he would repeat them. She came to the part that said, *"and forgive us our trespasses, as we forgive those who trespass against us".* But what the boy repeated was, *"and forgive us our trash baskets, as we forgive those who put trash in our baskets."* Well, that certainly brings clarity to the phrase, doesn't it!

When people hurt us, and notice I said **when**, not **if**, because all of us are vulnerable to being hurt by others, we become angry. Anger is a self-protective device. Anger says, "I'm not letting any more of this get in. I am already hurt enough. You will not hurt me again. I will hurt you back if I have to." Anger is the wall we build around our own wounded hearts. There is actually nothing wrong with getting angry, because it is a survival instinct, and initially we need to self-protect and step back to review the situation. People who are ashamed of feeling angry turn their emotions inward. They may say, "I'm not mad," while their stomachs are churning and their heads are beginning to pound. But whether we manifest it inwardly or outwardly, we all have anger when we are hurt.

THE WORLD'S METHOD OF DEALING WITH HURT

Many "experts" in the world will say that it is important for us to manifest our anger outwardly. The movies and TV set examples of "letting it all fly" verbally and physically. It is no wonder that our country has such a high incidence of domestic violence. We learn from the media to always stick the blame somewhere and "make 'em pay". They suggest that if authorities don't take the proper vengeance, there is some kind of honor in taking the law into your own hands, making you a hero. The world tells us that if you can't get away with throwing a tantrum, then just withdraw and have a "pity party". Hold the grudge and get even when you can, if not physically, then silently in your mind. Anger becomes trash in our baskets.

We all know that these methods of dealing with anger are a lie from the enemy of our souls, and will lead to depression or violence. In this way, the angry person goes into blame and unforgiveness, acts out, ends up hurting others, and reaps more hurt from the other's angry reaction. Being hurt again, he is back at the beginning of the cycle, and he begins to spiral upward in the intensity of negative emotion each time he has to deal with anger. When the cycle is continuous over a long period, anger brings in all of his friends.... bitterness, resentment, fear, unbelief, rejection... and the list goes on. The invasion of negativity brings about chemical changes in the brain, causing depression and mental problems, or physical illness.

Dealing with your anger the world's way can kill you!

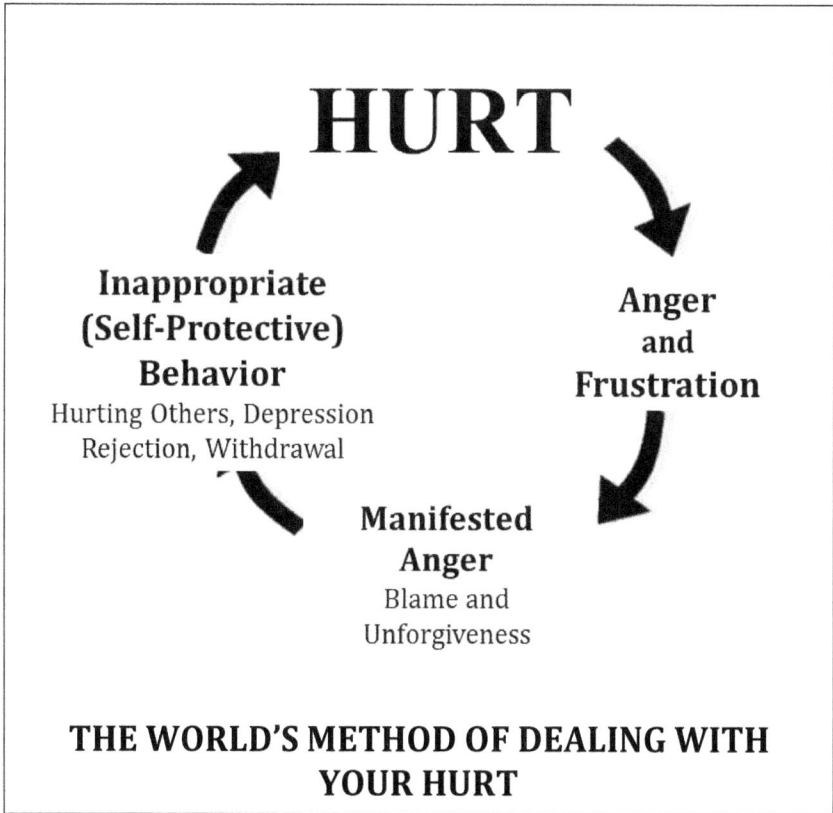

HURT

Inappropriate (Self-Protective) Behavior
Hurting Others, Depression
Rejection, Withdrawal

Anger and Frustration

Manifested Anger
Blame and
Unforgiveness

THE WORLD'S METHOD OF DEALING WITH YOUR HURT

GOD'S METHOD OF DEALING WITH YOUR HURT

The Lord has given us a much more practical plan! We **will** get hurt, and because we hurt, we **will** get angry, because no one is immune to getting hurt! But, the apostle Paul said,

> *Be angry, but do not sin.*
> *Do not let the sun go down on your wrath*
> *Do not give place to the devil. Ephesians 4:26*

In other words we might say, "Go ahead and get mad, but then... seek God's plan." Remember that "sin" is "missing the mark" of God's plan. And don't procrastinate, because if you wait too long to implement God's plan, the devil will have ample opportunity to get in, cause you to act out in ways that will hurt others and bring more hurt to yourself, and build a stronghold in your heart.

So what is God's strategy for dealing with anger? It is James 4: 7-12.

> *Therefore, submit to God.*

This means, be humble! Lay yourself down under the pattern! Seek Him and His perfect will, and acknowledge His authority over you! Admit that you don't know it all!

Resist the devil, and he will flee from you.

Tell the devil that he has no legal right to harass or torment you, that you are covered by the blood of Jesus. Rebuke his efforts to put thoughts of retaliation into your mind. Rebuke all lying spirits that cause you to think negative things about the other person. Remind the devil that you are God's loved child, filled with His Spirit, and that you operate in love, joy, and peace.

> *Draw near to God, and He will draw near to you.*

Begin to praise God for His goodness and mercy, and for using this negative situation to bring glory to His name. Thank Him for His word that promises, *all things work together for good for those who love God and are called according to His purposes (Romans 8:28)* and that *God inhabits the praises of His people (Psalm 22:3).* When you draw near to Him in praise and thanksgiving, He will draw near to you in comfort and strength.

> *Cleanse your hands, you sinners, and purify your hearts, you double-minded. Lament and mourn and weep! Let your laughter be turned to mourning and your joy to gloom. Humble yourself in the sight of the Lord and He will lift you up.*

Again, this is a call to humility. If you had any part in this circumstance that is making you angry, you will need to repent. Don't take on any false guilt, but if you are reacting negatively, be honest with God and ask for forgiveness. He will then be the "lifter of your head" and bring you out of your bitterness.

> Do not speak evil of one another, brethren. He who speaks evil of a brother and judges a brother, speaks evil of the law and judges the law. But if you judge the law, you are not a doer of the law but a judge. There is one Lawgiver, who is able to save and to destroy. Who are you to judge another?

If you are speaking evil of someone, either out loud or in your heart, you are judging. Judging is sin, and sin will put you back into darkness. God is the only one wise enough to judge with perfect justice. So, release the guilty party from your judgment and forgive!

A Hebrew word for forgive, *nasa*, (yes, just like the space agency) means *to "lift, advance, arise, bear up, bring forth, pardon, raise up"*. Use your imagination here. Pick up that person who hurt you and see God's hand coming down to meet you. Put that person in God's hand and watch Him take that person up and away. Let go!

The Greek word for forgiveness, *aphesis*, means *"freedom, pardon, deliverance, liberty"*. When you set this person free, God begins to go to work on his heart, and you have set yourself free from the burden of their sin. However, when you are judging them, you are chained to them and their sin. When you set them free, **you** are free!

Now God's comfort and healing can enable you to go on with life without resorting to bad behavior that would trap you back into the cycle of anger and pain. Your reward will be a peace that is not of this world!

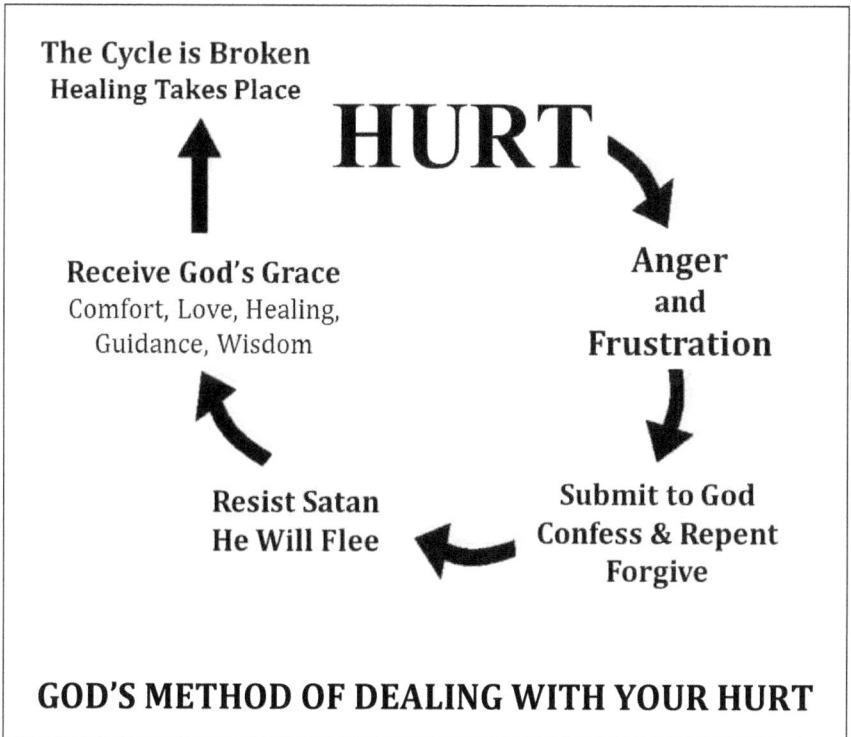

The Cycle is Broken
Healing Takes Place

HURT

Receive God's Grace
Comfort, Love, Healing,
Guidance, Wisdom

Anger
and
Frustration

Resist Satan
He Will Flee

Submit to God
Confess & Repent
Forgive

GOD'S METHOD OF DEALING WITH YOUR HURT

There have been times when I could not actually identify the source of my anger or figure out where the hurt was coming from. Sometimes we have so many emotions about so many things, that we begin to "stuff" them to get rid of them. But emotion cannot be stuffed permanently. Eventually, it will manifest as irritation, then anger, roaring out like a volcano in inappropriate ways, because emotions have to be processed. God helps us to sort out people and situations that need to be forgiven and washed in the blood of Jesus, and to show us where we need Him to touch our broken hearts and heal. So if I find myself feeling irritable and angry, I do a little exercise that the Lord has taught me. He says to me, *"Would you **give** Me your anger and let me hold it for a little while so I can show you the hurt and why it is there? Later, you can have it back if you want it!"* So I see His hand come down and I mentally give over my anger to Him, and then, if I stay still, He begins to help me sort things out. Of course, I never want my anger back later!

I have another visual that helps me to release hurtful people to God. When I hurt, I may think, "*I don't want to let this person off the hook.*" And I "see" a coat hook next to me and mentally hang that person on the hook! In that place I could berate them, blame them, and spew venom on them... but instead... I "see" God's great coat hook in the sky, and I take them off *my* hook, and put them on *God's* hook. I say, *"You take care of them, Lord! I am not their judge, so I release them to You!"* You see, since God contends with those who contend with us, and what they sow is what they reap, and God will bring them to repentance by His goodness, I know that God will handle the situation very well all by Himself, and I can let them go.

OTHER CAUSES OF ANGER

FEAR

Remembering that anger is a "protective wall", it is logical that fear can trigger our anger. When we perceive that our loved ones are going to be hurt, or we are going to be hurt, that fear prompts us to act out in anger. A parent who finds evidence that his child is on drugs may become very angry. But that kind of anger is not always a bad emotion. It stirs us to action and gives us the boldness we need to handle the situation. The key, again, is to be humble enough to submit ourselves and the situation to God, resisting the devil and reminding him that he has no authority, and drawing near to God, so that He can give us direction. If there is another person involved in the situation who is contributing to your fear, **forgive** that one and continue to wash him in forgiveness so that God has a clear path to reach him. **ONLY GOD IS GOING TO SOLVE YOUR PROBLEM.** If you try to solve it with your own limited knowledge and strength, you will make matters worse.

In this age of economic instability, crime, political unrest, and all of the woes of the world, some people are angry all the time because of their fear and the things they "perceive" are going to happen. They become militant and controlling, not out of the guidance of God, but out of worry for their own personal safety or the safety of their loved ones. We cannot live in peace and rest when fear has taken hold, and the authority that God gives us to bring change only operates out of a soul in peace. Public criticism of government and authority figures brings more judgment and darkness over the very ones in authority that could serve us more efficiently if those authorities were receiving wisdom from God. Forgive those who are making wrong decisions and bathe them in prayer, that God will give them visions and dreams and change their hearts! He is able to guide them in a new direction supernaturally, if we will cooperate with the Spirit.

Constant anxiety in a person suggests a need for some deep inner healing of past hurts. But in dealing with fears as they come, I find these scriptures to be very soothing to my soul:

> *Be anxious for nothing, but in everything by prayer and supplication, with thanksgiving, let your request be made known to God; and the peace that passes all understanding will guard your hearts and minds through Christ Jesus. Philippians 4: 6-7*

Cast all your care upon Him, for He cares for you. I Peter 5:7

For God has not given us a spirit of fear, but of power and of love and of a sound mind.

II Timothy 1:7

FRUSTRATION

Frustration is the emotion we feel when we are thwarted in getting what we want or need in our expected time frame. It is accompanied by a fear that we will never get what we planned on, and it often brings up a lot of anger. Sometimes we are frustrated by our own inability to make things happen, and that becomes unforgiveness toward ourselves. Sometimes other people ruin our plans, ignore our needs, or just don't hear us, and we find ourselves judging them. And then, it is very frustrating when people we love are doing things that will harm themselves, when we have worked hard to give them a life of success! In all of these cases, the anger we feel can be handled, just as we explained before. When we humble ourselves before God and stop striving to make things happen, God steps in to take over.

I love this poem by Lauretta P. Burns....

> *As children bring their broken toys, with tears, for us to mend,*
>
> *I brought my broken dreams to God, because He was my friend.*
>
> *But then, instead of leaving Him in peace to work alone,*
>
> *I hung around and tried to help in ways that were my own.*
>
> *At last, I grabbed them back and cried, "How could You be so slow?"*
>
> *"My child", He said. "What could I do? You never did let go!"*

The danger in allowing disappointment to overtake us is that we begin to murmur against God, as though He doesn't know what He is doing or as though He doesn't care! That unforgiveness toward God is a closed door to God's grace, and an open door to a spirit of unbelief.

Once we truly submit to God's way of doing things without grumbling and complaining, we find we are growing more fruits in the Spirit and moving up a level in our Christian walk. Peace. Gentleness. Patience. Learning to see life through God's eyes. He is always working for the best outcome for everyone in terms of eternal value, which may not match our desire for instant answers. Humility is willingness to admit that you may not see the whole picture, but God, in His wisdom, always does!

INJUSTICE

Injustice is a big anger producer! We have an inbuilt aversion to things that are "not fair" or "not right". I am angry when I see things being shown on television that corrupt the minds of our young people. I am angry when I see our government passing laws that will ultimately destroy the moral fiber of our country. I am angry that unborn babies are being murdered because they are not convenient. Jesus was angry when He saw the moneychangers defiling His Father's temple. Scripture records that He threw them out - but it does not record that people were injured. He hated the sin, but loved the sinners. We must be very careful what we do with our **righteous anger**. Again, always begin with forgiveness. Fast and pray and wait on the Lord, and do not jump into action. Wait until you have direction from Him, with several confirmations from the word of God and reliable spiritual authorities. Some of us are called to act and some of us are called to intercede. Know where the Lord is placing you, and stay under His authority! God can change any situation, and even great injustice often serves the purposes of God. Wasn't the death of Jesus the ultimate injustice? Yet God used it to bring about the redemption of all mankind. If we will praise

Him, even in the unfair situations of life, He will redeem and restore and bring victory.

Many things will happen to us in our own lives that are "not fair". Sudden crisis in a family, the death of loved ones, abandonment of a spouse, false accusations turned against us, the loss of provision or health, the list is endless. God is not blind and deaf to your situation! As you turn over the "broken dream" to God and **let go**, He will turn what the devil meant for evil into something good. He knows our woundedness, and He is always there to bring healing and wholeness. Life is not fair. Don't expect it to be fair. Just expect God to show up!

TYPES OF UNFORGIVENESS WE SOMETIMES DON'T RECOGNIZE

GUILTY SHAME

There are two types of shame. The first is a shame caused by guilt when you have actually sinned. That is easy to handle!

> *If you confess your sins, God is faithful to forgive your sins and cleanse you from all unrighteousness. I John 1:9*

You confess it, the blood of Jesus washes it away. End of story.

Unfortunately, the devil enjoys dredging up our old sins to remind us over and over how bad we are. Allowing him to do that is a waste of your life. Jesus was tortured beyond belief, and suffered a horrible death, so that you would never have to suffer for your sin, but could be instantly forgiven and back in fellowship with the Father. Living with guilt and mentally punishing yourself over and over is an insult to the One who died for you. And it serves no purpose.

This little story has been a favorite of mine. Although the author is unknown, it is a perfect example of the uselessness of self-condemnation.

A little boy named Johnny and his sister, Susie, were spending the summer with their grandparents on their farm. Johnny, with his new slingshot, was practicing his aim in the woods next to the barnyard. He was not hitting anything he aimed for, which were mainly trees, and felt very discouraged as he walked back to the barn. Grandma's favorite duck waddled by. Without even thinking, Johnny raised the slingshot, let the rock fly, and whaaap! It hit the duck, and the duck keeled over, quite dead! Johnny was horrified. Seeing a woodpile nearby, he removed a few pieces and stuffed the body of the duck under the pile. Just then, he heard a movement behind him, and there was his sister Susie, watching intently, with a very evil grin on her face. She did not say a word, but walked away smiling.

That evening after dinner, Grandpa said, "While you girls are cleaning up, Johnny and I are going downtown to do an errand, and probably stop for an ice cream on the way home." Susie spoke up, "Oh, but Grandpa, Johnny said he was going to do the dishes for me tonight! I'll be glad to go with you instead!" And out of the side of her mouth she whispered to Johnny, "Remember the duck?" So Johnny ended up not only doing the dishes that night, but was blackmailed into doing all of Susie's chores, as well as his own, for the next three days.

Finally, exhausted and frustrated and angry, Johnny decided to confess. He went to his Grandma and said, "Grandma, I'm so sorry! I killed your favorite duck!"

His Grandma looked at him lovingly and replied, "I know you did, Johnny. I was standing at the window and I saw you do it. But I forgave you right away when you did it."

Johnny was appalled. "Grandma! **Why didn't you tell me?***"*

And Grandma replied, "Well, I just wanted to see how long you would let your sister hold you hostage."

Remember, whenever you sin, Jesus is well aware of what you have done, and He forgives you. But you have to appropriate that forgiveness for yourself by confessing it. And then it is over! Don't let the devil hold you hostage!

IDENTITY SHAME

This type of shame is actually unforgiveness against your own identity. It is believing yourself to be defective, flawed, inadequate, ineffectual, less than… that you don't measure up. Measure up to what? Ah… measure up to the world's standards! You're not as smart… as good looking…. as influential… as affluent as… as what? As others that you know or have heard of. You have made a comparison and come out wanting! Who on earth put the idea in your mind that you should be compared to others? The devil, of course! God never compares you to anyone, because you have been uniquely designed. You are one of a kind, created to be born at this time for purposes on the earth that only God knows. You are His special weapon against the works of the enemy. The enemy knows this, and if he can deceive you into believing that you don't measure up, he can sabotage God's work through you. He likes to remind you of your inadequacies and get you blaming yourself for your failure to measure up to the "good Christian" stereotype.

What does the Truth tell us about this?

> *I will praise You, for I am fearfully and wonderfully made; marvelous are Your works, and that my soul knows very well.*
> *Psalms 139:14*

You are exactly the way God made you for His purposes, and He accepts you and approves you just the way you are!

> *For we dare not class ourselves or compare ourselves with those who commend themselves. But they, measuring themselves by themselves, and comparing themselves among themselves, are not wise.* *II Corinthians 10: 12*

So don't listen to the media about what you "should be". Don't look at others with assets that you don't have and compare yourself with them! The Lord once said to me, "*Why do you want to be a mountain when I have made you to be a beautiful babbling brook?*" He clearly wanted me to accept who I am and to praise Him for making me the way He liked me!

Now look at this next scripture:

> *Now, therefore, you are no longer strangers and foreigners, but fellow citizens with the saints and members of the household of God, having been built on the foundation of the apostles and prophets, Jesus Christ being the chief cornerstone, in whom the whole*

building, being joined together, grows into a holy temple in the Lord, in whom you also are being built together for a habitation of God in the Spirit. Ephesians 2:19-22

We are joined together like "puzzle pieces"! Where I am weak, you come along beside me with your giftings, your strength, your calling, and we fit together. Where I am strong, I come along beside someone who is weak with my giftings, strength, and calling, and we fit together. And their strength in some area will click together with someone else's weakness....and so on as we are built together into a united habitation of the Spirit. This is God's plan for the Bride of Christ: Everyone taking his place in the Body of Christ, living within their own limitations so that others can take their place in the Body. No one pretending they are what they aren't and pushing into another's space. No one hanging back and leaving a space! It is a supernatural building being erected one soul at a time. This is why we must forgive ourselves for being "less than", which is a lie, wipe away the shame and take our honored position in the House of God.

UNREALISTIC EXPECTATIONS

We owe God a great debt for what He has done for us. There is no way for us to repay that debt of agape love, perfectly loving God and loving others. But the Lord has forgiven us for our inability to pay that debt.

Yet, we often hold onto our expectations of others, believing that they should pay their debt of love to us in full. When we hold them accountable to meeting our expectations, we set them up for failure. Then, when we are disappointed, we use that excuse to judge them. God accepts us just as we are, warts and all! The heart of God within us will accept the people around us, even when they are being unlovely. God is pleased when we submit to His desires and release them from their debt. Better yet, to not have unrealistic expectations to start with, but allow each person to be who they are becoming. They are "under construction" by God just as we are. We are blind to God's greater blessings when our outlook is limited to our own expectations. God doesn't zap people immediately when we pray, because He is more interested in the process than the outcome. The process of making them all He wants them to be is also the process of growing the fruits of the Spirit in you! Keep them under construction by washing them in the blood of Jesus, and watch them change! Put your expectation in God alone and watch what He does with you!

GOSSIP

Gossip is contagious unforgiveness! If you become offended at someone's actions, you have just fallen into the devil's trap! The word "offended" in the Greek is "*scandalizo*", which means "to entrap, trip up, entice to sin, or stumble". Be on guard. When people disrespect you, don't give you credit when credit is due, and pass you over for someone else, it is easy to be "offended". You can get out of the trap right there by forgiving and blessing. But if you don't, you are in danger of telling others what was done to you. Words, and even thoughts, have energy and power. If others pick up your offense, they are in danger of passing the story along, even in a prayer group. Many people may pick up the offense and begin judging the offender. Heaven closes up, God's grace is cut off, not only for the offender, but for all those judging him. All this can be prevented by forgiving the original offense before it became contagious! Sometimes you may need a trusted friend with whom you can vent your feelings, but you must always choose a person who understands the problems associated with taking on an offense. Someone who will help you process and come to the place of forgiveness. Someone mature in the faith who will not judge.

On one occasion, a person I thought highly of betrayed me. I went through the process of forgiveness. However, in conversations with friends I kept going back to the story of the betrayal. I heard the Spirit in my heart say, "If you've really forgiven, why are you talking about it?" When God forgives, He actually forgets the sin. We need to do likewise.

In these "end times", we must be aware that the enemy will always try to block us from God's blessing by setting up situations where we will be offended. Offense is truly the "bait of satan". The Bride of Christ must become **unoffendable** if she is to stay in a place of God's power and authority.

MURMURING AND COMPLAINING

There are multitudes of things we could complain about in this life. But doing so is like saying, "God is not good enough for me. He is not watching over me. He doesn't care." Murmuring and complaining is unforgiveness against God. Again, that barrier of sin stands between us, and then we are unable to **see** the good things that God **is** doing or the good things that people are doing for us! This is what He tells us through the apostle Paul:

> Beloved do not think it strange concerning the fiery trial which is to try you, as though some strange thing happened to you; but rejoice to the extent that you partake of Christ's sufferings, that when His glory is revealed, you also may be glad with exceeding joy. I Peter 4:12-13

Let us not forget the Israelites who started out on an 11 day trip to the Promised Land. Because of their constant murmuring and complaining, the Lord was not able to bring them into the Promised Land, where they would need the Lord's strategy to defeat their enemies. For 40 years they wandered in the wilderness, as God tried to show them His faithfulness. But the sin of complaining against God blinded them to God's goodness and they died in the wilderness. Hopefully, we have learned something from their example!

GENERATIONAL INIQUITY

When Israel rebelled against God in the wilderness, Moses stood and interceded for the people. In Numbers 14:17-19 he prayed,

> *And now, I pray, let the power of my Lord be great, just as You have spoken, saying, "The Lord is long-suffering and abundant in mercy, forgiving iniquity and transgression; but He by no means clears the guilty, **visiting the iniquity of the fathers on the children to the third and fourth generation."** Pardon the iniquity of this people, I pray, according to the greatness of Your mercy, just as You have forgiven this people, from Egypt even until now.*

I did not get a clear understanding of this until I read a passage from an old classic called ***Maximized Manhood*** by Edwin L. Cole. The story he related was one of a man who wanted prayer for his alcoholic sons. It became apparent that he himself had been an alcoholic and had never openly asked his sons for forgiveness. Dr. Cole agreed to pray with him on the condition that he would go to his sons and do this immediately. As the author puts it,

> *In forgiving someone's sins we release them, but when we do not forgive them, those sins are retained. It is a Kingdom principle. That man's sons hated his alcoholism. They never forgave him for it. Because they never forgave him, they retained their father's sin and became like the thing they hated. Hate binds it to you. They bound themselves to their father's sin.*

What an eye opener this was for me! All sin must be covered by the shed blood of Jesus to cleanse the defilement of iniquity upon the future generations of our families. I hope that you will take the time to root out the sin problems of past generations in your own family history. You can apply the blood of Jesus in forgiveness and break the generational curses that have come down your family line. What sins are you seeing in your children and grandchildren? Of course, you are to forgive them, but perhaps you will also need to go to them in humility and ask for forgiveness for the very same sin in you, knowing that this simple act will break the power of satan over future generations.

EXCUSES WE USE FOR NOT FORGIVING!

How we love to justify our rebellion against God! Here are some common excuses for refusing to forgive:

1. **They hurt me too much.**
   These are the words of someone who has a backlog of pain that needs inner healing and a spirit of self-pity. This person will have to seek some healing and deliverance to get free, and to make the decision to be "powerful" rather than "pitiful" for the Kingdom of God!

2. **They are not sorry.**
   Luke 17: 3-4 tells us that if our offender repents, we should forgive. Certainly! But it does not say that we do **not** need to forgive if he **doesn't** repent! Some people use that scripture to justify holding onto their judgment, but the scriptures we looked at earlier are telling us to forgive, whether they repent or not.

3. **They keep doing this to me over and over.**
   Matthew 18: 21-22 tells us to keep forgiving, 70 x 7 if we need to! This does not mean that we just stand there and take it over and over. It means that as we continue to wash this person in the blood of Jesus, we also seek the Lord about what type of boundaries He would have us put into operation. God does not want you continually hurt. He will give you a strategy to

get through this. In the next chapter we will discuss times of separation, trust, and reconciliation.

4. **If I forgive them, I will have to treat them right.**
Absolutely! If God has forgiven your sin and forgotten it and treats you as though it had never happened...then you must do the same!

5. **They have to be punished or they won't ever stop.**
Actually, the opposite is true. Listen to these scriptures:

*Or do you despise the riches of His goodness, forbearance, and longsuffering, not knowing that **the goodness of God** leads you to repentance? Romans 2:4*

Therefore, if your enemy hungers, feed him; if he thirsts, give him a drink; for in doing so you will heap coals of fire on his head. Do not be overcome by evil, but overcome evil with good. Romans 12:20-21

When you blame a person and act out your disapproval, the offender's heart hardens against you and the situation escalates. If you forgive and treat the offender with respect and understanding, God's power brings conviction to the offender. God's goodness, working through you, will lead him to repentance.

6. **I just can't do it.**
   We discussed earlier the formation of demonic strongholds in the soul. A person who has lived his life with a critical, unforgiving spirit for many years may need to see a prayer minister to break the stronghold of unforgiveness and get some inner healing.

7. **They had a hard life, so I'll just excuse them.**
   NO!! Excusing is not the same as forgiving! Excusing is just covering up the sin. God desires that all sin be exposed and permanently washed away in the blood of Jesus. Sin has to be recognized as sin. The offender needs conviction, so that he has an opportunity to repent and come into the loving presence of God. Jesus died for us all. God's love and forgiveness, flowing through us, can bring many into the Kingdom!

UNBELIEF

One reason we don't follow through with our forgiveness strategy is because we don't really believe in our heart that it will do any good! We forget that unbelief is a spirit that comes to blind us to the power that we hold within us from the Holy Spirit. When we stay in the Word of God and surround ourselves with believers that encourage us in the faith, we will not succumb to the strategy of the enemy! Smith Wigglesworth (1859-1947) was a powerful evangelist and healer who is still a great encouragement to us today. In the book, **SMITH WIGGLESWORTH ON SPIRITUAL GIFTS** he says, *"Some of you have come from your homes with broken hearts; you have a longing for something to strengthen you in the midst of the conditions that exist there, and a power to make these conditions different. You say you are 'unequally yoked together with unbelievers' (II Cor. 6:14). You have a mighty power that is greater than all natural power. You can take victory over your homes and your spouses and children, and **you must do it in the Lord's way**. Suppose you do see many things that ought to be different; if it is your cross, you must take it and win the victory for God. It can be done, for He who is in you is greater than all the power of hell. (I John 4:4). I believe that anyone filled with the Holy Spirit is equal to a legion of demons any day."*

The Lord's way that he is speaking of is the way of forgiveness and believing and applying the power of the blood of Jesus! Never give up! No matter how long it takes, keep the forgiveness flowing until you see the breakthrough, and then keep forgiving after that. You will see the power of God manifest to give you the victory!

CHAPTER 10
TO RECONCILE OR NOT TO RECONCILE

If we say we forgive and yet decline opportunities for reconciliation with the forgiven party, have we really forgiven? It is easy to speak forgiveness in our minds and then call it "done", but to actually reach out and contact the person we have forgiven to repair the breach is a much more difficult act requiring the stripping away of personal pride. Forgiveness is love. Forgiveness is the atoning and remitting power of the blood of Jesus.

> *And above all, have fervent love for one another, for love will **cover** a multitude of sins. I Peter 4:8*

The word "reconciliation" in the Greek, *katallage,* is also translated *atonement,* which means "*to cover*". Forgiveness without any effort toward reconciliation is not complete forgiveness. However, even if you are ready to reconcile, the other party may not feel the same way. Love is waiting for that person to become ready for reconciliation, which, in some cases, may be a matter of years. You continue to wash that person in forgiveness and to remain open to reconciliation until the breach is repaired, no matter how long that takes.

When you have been rejected in your efforts to reconcile, it is very difficult to risk another rejection. This is all a part of *loving not our lives unto death.* Dying to our own self-protective devices will bring God's resurrection power and restoration into a broken relationship. A humble repairer of the breach is pleasing in the sight of God.

ABUSIVE RELATIONSHIPS

Sometimes there needs to be a separation in a relationship in order to break the cycle of abuse, whether it be physical or emotional. People who are very emotionally wounded can also become very abusive. Making the decision to leave an abusive person can be difficult. But if there is any type of physical abuse, or if children are being physically or emotionally abused, it is wise to remove yourself and children from that dangerous situation. If you are considering this, seek reliable spiritual counsel. God does **NOT** want you to put yourself in harm's way. However, His plan always includes washing the offender in the blood of Jesus and praying blessings over that person, so that he has the opportunity to see his own sin, repent, and change. In your own relationship with the Lord, you will want to get His direction about whether you need to separate, when, and how it should be done. You may need inner healing to help you avoid the tendency to "replay tapes" in your head, blaming the offender. Or to avoid minimizing the seriousness of the situation and excusing rather than forgiving the offender. Stay focused on the goal... forgive... God wants to get through. Keep heaven open with the washing of Jesus' blood! And releasing the offender to God will take a burden off your own soul! Sometimes it is actually easier to forgive someone who isn't around you every day re-opening old wounds. The Lord will want to spend time with you, giving you rest, comfort and healing, as He wraps His loving arms around you. He will heal your broken heart and give you continued strength for the battle to bring your offender into the light. Listen for God's voice to tell you when it is safe to restore relationship.

RECONCILIATION

I separated myself from God for many years, and He repeatedly forgave me and made numerous attempts to reconcile with me. Yet I was not "ready" to really be reconciled to Him until I was over thirty years of age. He is longsuffering and faithful, and He never stops looking for the moment when His prodigal child returns to relationship. He always desires that hearts will be healed and changed, and we can be reconciled with Him and each other. But reconciliation is a process of reestablishing **trust,** which takes time and patience and the guidance of the Lord. Wisdom tells us that certain steps must be taken:

1. The offender must demonstrate genuine repentance.
2. He must acknowledge that he has caused great harm.
3. He must do what is necessary to make amends.
4. He must be willing to submit to boundaries set by the victim.

I suggest that you read more on this subject in the **Boundaries** series of books by Henry Cloud and John Townsend. Information on three of these books can be found at the back of this publication in the References and Resources section.

Boundaries for the offender may include getting inner healing, seeing a counselor, or entering a program for alcohol or drug abuse. Setting boundaries is crucial, because if you allow the offender to continue to hurt you, you are contributing to his sin by being an "enabler". Offenders don't change when enablers allow them to continue to sin, and their lack of repentance keeps them separated from God. Also, enabling an offender keeps you stuck as a victim instead of a victor!

The important thing, no matter how long it takes or what specific steps are implemented, is that you keep the forgiveness going for your own sake and for the offender's sake. And since God does not put limits on the time it takes us to reconcile with Him, we should not put limits on the time it takes the offender to reconcile.

Sometimes we have so much built-up anger and mistrust that we just want to write off the whole relationship, believing that the other person will never change. Everyone is capable of change when God gets ahold of their heart! Even if you can't trust the offender, you can trust God *with* the offender. Let God heal your heart and keep your mind open to the possibility of change in your offender's heart.

Also, consider that because of your own woundedness, you may be contributing to the relationship problems. You may have been afraid of confrontation and remained silent in the face of difficulties until you were totally fed up and wanted to throw in the towel! But relationships require the courage to face problem areas and find resolution. If you have been critical or judgmental, like I was, or self-righteously opinionated, or self-focused because of your inner pain, then you will need to humbly allow God to show you how you have hurt your offender. Then follow the steps of wisdom yourself!

One other thought... if you do reconcile, give up the expectation that the other person is going to "follow the rules" perfectly! Such expectation will only bring you disappointment. Applaud the times that the person succeeds and forgive the times he doesn't. As

God forgives you in your imperfect state, you forgive them also. God's grace is sufficient for both of you.

CHAPTER 11
THE HIGH CALLING OF GOD

Forgiveness becomes a natural part of everyday life when we are "abiding" in God.

> *I am the vine, you are the branches. He who abides in Me, and I in him, bears much fruit; for without Me you can do nothing. John 15:5*

> *By this My Father is glorified, that you bear much fruit; so you will be My disciples. As the Father loved Me, I also have loved you; abide in My love. John 15:8-9*

In every negative circumstance, we should be so filled with God's heart that we use that situation to God's advantage by praying the blood of Jesus over every person involved. We change the atmosphere as we walk in authority, applying the blood as priests to our God.

We discussed earlier the fact that we, as Christians, may be assaulted by satan in order to stop our progress. And like Peter, in Luke 22: 31, God may even allow satan a period of "sifting us like wheat" to prove our faithfulness and durability. But we must remember that satan cannot do anything to a Christian **unless the Lord allows it.** Why would the Lord allow bad things to happen to His chosen ones?

Why did God allow Jesus to suffer and die on the cross?
THAT ALL MEN MIGHT BE REDEEMED AND DRAWN BACK INTO FELLOWSHIP WITH THE FATHER.

Every place a Christian walks, then, because of the power and authority of the Holy Spirit within him, is an opportunity for God to draw more men unto Him. Many unbelievers have no friends or family members who will pray for them and ask God to forgive them of their sins. They have no chance of being released from their prison of darkness until someone with the Holy Spirit forgives them. If God would send His only Son to die so that we might be released from satan's power, would He not send us into perilous situations also, that we would pull others out of the grasp of the devil? The very situations that we are apt to complain about in our lives are the situations that God has allowed for the redemption of some person's soul. **It is time that Christians begin to view the unfortunate things that happen to them in the light of eternal significance rather than in the light of their own comfort.**

I have a friend, Donna, who has a sweet, forgiving spirit, because she walks so closely with the Lord. One day it was raining in torrents and a young man ran into the back of her car. He was terribly concerned that she would call the police, because he had alcohol on his breath. Her tire had flattened, so he set about changing it, hoping it would give him favor. For nearly an hour, he struggled in the rain. Donna, of course, was praying, and expected that a police car might stop by. However, no police car ever arrived. God's still small voice gave her a word of knowledge and a direction:

He is addicted to alcohol and drugs.
Administer salvation.

Donna had already forgiven the young man in her heart. She said to him, "The Lord says that He will heal you of your addiction to alcohol and drugs if you will give your life over to Him."

Repentant tears flowed with the rain as he prayed to receive Jesus into his heart.

And what about the damage done? Insurance paid for part, and Donna received extra clients at work to pay for the rest. God redeems and restores when we freely allow Him to use us for His work. Even if He had not covered the cost of the damage, Donna would have been joyful, because she had done the Father's will.

Many of you have suffered things that are much worse than having your car smashed. But God loves us all so much that He will allow many adverse circumstances in order to bring all men into His Kingdom. I am not saying that God caused this accident. I am saying that

God will USE what satan has meant for evil to bring about His own purposes.

One of the most difficult things to forgive is ritual abuse suffered by a child. Young ones who are tortured often see into the spirit world. A dear friend named Ann is one of those who was abused in this way. Even as a child, she had a choice to hate her abusers or forgive. When Ann's hate and anger began to manifest as she was brutally tortured, she could see demons growing in size and power. Conversely, when she made the choice to forgive, she saw angels being energized and great light growing and consuming the darkness. It was a choice to empower heaven or hell.

One of the after effects of this abuse was the fear of authority figures and the tendency to respond in fear and rage inwardly toward them, when they made poor decisions. But one day, as an adult, when she was taking communion, a sudden realization came to her that Jesus died for the sins of those evil ones who abused children. And Jesus died for the sins of authority figures who made poor decisions. A tsunami of God's love and forgiveness washed over her, as she could see it washing over the abusers and a present authority figure she was struggling with. All of the effects of abuse washed away, and she felt relief and freedom. Interestingly, the situation with the authority figure completely changed after that, and

Ann was repositioned to a place where she is free to use her gifts.

She related this story of forgiveness to a friend who had an unlovable neighbor, and as her friend forgave, the neighbor's actions entirely changed. The blessings of God spread like ripples in a lake when someone forgives and opens heaven!

Choosing to love and forgive in the midst of great darkness produces exponentially greater light. Each pound of sacrifice yields a massive harvest of blessing!

Note: We do have a choice in our attitude toward difficult circumstances. I believe that if a Christian continually gripes and complains about adversity, God will move on to someone else to carry out His work. We miss out on great joy when we have the wrong attitude. If we view the hurtful incidents of the past with a bitter spirit it causes us to see the whole world around us with negativity. We will expect bad things to happen to us, which becomes a self-fulfilling prophesy. The devil is glad to accommodate us when we have negative expectations. People who know that God loves them are looking and expecting good things from Him and know that "*all things are working together for their good*" (Romans 8:28). They are constantly giving thanks for every situation that comes their way. Then thanksgiving takes them into the presence of God... "*Enter into His gates with thanksgiving and into His courts with praise. Be thankful to Him and bless His name."* (Psalm 100:4) ...and the Presence of God walks them through even the most difficult trials in perfect peace.

The apostle Paul is such a good example to us in facing trials for the sake of the gospel! He said in Hebrews 12:3,

> *Consider Him who endured such hostility from sinners against Himself, lest you become weary and discouraged in your souls.*

And in II Timothy 2:10,

> *Therefore, I endure all things for the sake of the elect, that they also may obtain the salvation which is in Christ Jesus with eternal glory.*

And in James 1:2,

> *My brethren, count it all joy when you fall into various trials.*

And in Philippians 4:4,

> *Rejoice in the Lord always, and again I will say, rejoice!*

Next time you find yourself in a situation, whether good or bad, just ask,

- Am I here to extend God's forgiveness to someone?

- Do I choose to empower demons or angels?

- Lord, what would you have me do for Your glory?"

Christianity is not for wimps! We have a high calling on our lives. Would you give to the Lord that which costs you nothing?

Jesus was born to forgive and die and be raised in resurrection power. We are born again to die to self and forgive and live in resurrection power. It is our reasonable service unto our Lord.

CHAPTER 12

NATIONS OF THE WORLD IN DARKNESS

Earlier we discussed the darkness over our nation, a result of the sin barrier between our nation and God. Not only is that barrier a result of the sin we perpetrate today, but it is also a result of the sin of generations past. Every strategy God gives us to set individuals free is one that can be used corporately for nations.

Individuals confess sin, repent, receive forgiveness and forgive others. Representatives of nations can also do the same. Over the last quarter of a century, this has been happening, but very slowly. God has given us the ministry of reconciliation, and this ministry is moving among the nations to bring the hearts of the nations back to God. Perhaps we can say that the ministry of reconciliation **is** the ministry of the Spirit of Elijah!

> *Now all things are of God who has reconciled us to Himself through Jesus Christ, and has given us the ministry of reconciliation, that is, that God was in Christ reconciling the world to Himself, not imputing their trespasses to them, and has committed to us the **word of reconciliation**. Therefore we are ambassadors for Christ, as though God were*

*pleading through us: we implore you on Christ's behalf, be **reconciled** to God.*
II Corinthians 5:18-20

*Behold, I will send you Elijah the prophet before the coming of the great and dreadful day of the Lord. And he will **turn the hearts of the fathers to the children, and the heart of the children to their fathers**, lest I come and strike the earth with a curse.*
Malachi 4:5-6

Elijah laid out the sacrifice, and the power of God opened the blind eyes of the people so that they would know the true God. Likewise, we, with the Spirit of Elijah, apply the blood of our perfect sacrifice, Jesus Christ, to tear down the barrier of sin between individuals and their God and between nations and their God.

IDENTIFICATIONAL REPENTANCE

How do we even begin to move a nation back to God? The Old Testament reveals over and over the sin cycle... how God prospers a nation, the people live in blessing for a period, but then begin to worship the blessings and not the One who blessed. They worship the creation but not the Creator. As sin takes hold, the barrier between the people and God grows thicker. Evil leaders take over. The nation collapses. Until...

the remnant of God's believers rise up to ask God's forgiveness for the nation to pull the sin barrier down.

If My people, who are called by My name will humble themselves and seek My face, and turn from their wicked ways, then I will hear from heaven, and will forgive their sin, and heal their land. II Chronicles 7:14

Identificational repentance happens when a believer repents on behalf of his own nation, including himself as a fellow sinner in the prayer. For instance, if I am asking God to forgive our nation for the sin of abortion, I include myself in the category of sinner, even though I, personally, have never had an abortion. I identify with the system I am a part of and repent on behalf of the whole system.

Nehemiah fasted and wept and mourned for his nation. He was identificationally repenting when he prayed,

*Please let Your ear be attentive and Your eyes open, that You may hear the prayer of Your servant which I pray before You now, day and night, for the children of Israel Your servants, and confess the sins of the children of Israel which **we** have sinned against You. Both **my father's house and I** have sinned. **We** have acted very corruptly against You and have not kept the commandments, the statutes, nor the*

*ordinances which You commanded Your
servant Moses. Nehemiah 1: 6-7*

Daniel was also an identificational repenter as he
sought the Lord for the forgiveness of his people:

> *And I prayed to the Lord my God, and made
> confession, and said, "O Lord, great and
> awesome God, who keeps His covenant and
> mercy with those who love Him, and with
> those who keep His commandments, **we** have
> sinned and committed iniquity, **we** have done
> wickedly and rebelled, even by departing from
> Your precepts and judgments. Daniel 9: 4-5*

C. Peter Wagner is a modern day apostle and prophet.
In an article from *Charisma* magazine he gives the
steps to this type of prayer:

1. Identify the national sin (racism, abortion,
   idolatry, etc.)
2. Confess the sin corporately and ask God for
   forgiveness.
3. Apply Christ's blood.
4. Walk in obedience and repair the damage.

The reason we can repent on behalf of anyone, is that
we recognize the iniquity that had come down on us
all, and we see that iniquity on ourselves, as well as
our nation. In essence, we are admitting that we are a

part of the sin problem. Of course, whatever personal sin we discover in ourselves must be dealt with also, as the condition the Lord has placed upon the healing of our land is that we "turn from our wicked ways". As we continue to forgive those who are still involved in sin, God will continue to give them revelation of their own sin, so that they also may "turn from their wicked ways".

To bring this closer to home, we can also repent on behalf of our families, our neighborhoods, our towns, cities, and states. Any group we are a part of, we can repent for! That includes our churches, our work places, our places of recreation; the list is endless. What blessings we will see, if we use this precious gift of God to break the power of sin!

PRAYER WALKING AND TERRAFORMING

Years ago, a prayer walk called Reconciliation Walk was organized in England to retrace the footsteps taken by the Crusaders for the purpose of reconciliation among Christians, Muslims, and Jews. Many other walks have taken place since that time, with intercessors applying the redeeming blood of Jesus where violence and evil have defiled the land, asking God for forgiveness. Prayer walking is something that all of us can do in our neighborhoods, around governmental buildings in our cities, states, and nation. There are many large Christian organizations that are now covering our governmental leaders in constant prayer, petitioning heaven for forgiveness and change of hearts and laws.

A movement called "Terraforming" purposes to "prepare creation for the Presence of God, dismantling the kingdom of darkness while establishing the dominion of God on earth." Again, this is done by going to places where sin has defiled the land and praying and redeeming the land by the blood of Jesus.

God has been raising up many ministries to get this work done on the earth before Jesus comes again! It is the Spirit of Elijah, taking back what the enemy has stolen, and ushering in a great revival that will cover the earth!

ONE NATION, ONE DAY

A couple of years ago a very energetic, on-fire-for-God young man named Dominic Russo came to our city to introduce the vision that God had given him to bring an entire nation to God in one day!

> *Who has heard such a thing? Who has seen such things? Shall the earth be made to give birth in one day? Or shall a nation be born at once? For as soon as Zion travailed, she gave birth to her children. Isaiah 66: 8*

Three years ago, Dominic took hundreds of volunteers into Honduras. With the permission of the government, he sent teams into every major city at the same time on the same day, doing crusades simultaneously in each place, bringing people to Christ. In one day, thousands accepted the Lord, and since then the nation has begun to prosper again.

This year on July 25, 2015, Dominic brought 2600 volunteers into the Dominican Republic. In the week before the crusade they brought medical teams, built new homes for the homeless, gave out shoes and even baseball gloves. They poured out prayer and love to the poverty stricken population. God did a miraculous work in physical and emotional healings and thousands of salvations. Of course, before Dominic even received the permission of government leaders, intercessors laid the groundwork, breaking through the darkness by the power of the Blood of Jesus. As they pulled that barrier down, God's light opened the door to that nation.

RELEASING THE CAPTIVES OF FALSE RELIGIONS

Jesus said, "I am the way, and the truth, and the life. No one comes to the Father except through Me." John 14: 6

Because Jesus was the sacrifice for sin that opened the Holy of Holies, each one of us must go through that blood to reach God. There are many "good" people in the world today, who do many "good" things, but have been deceived into putting their trust in other gods. The church invests a lot of money and time into missions to preach the gospel, and yes, the gospel must be preached! But blind eyes must be opened first, or the gospel falls on deaf ears.

Over the last few years many mission groups have joined prayer forces to focus on various people groups, researching their history and praying the blood of Jesus over the sins of the people. As they "prepare the way of the Lord" through repentance and forgiveness, the missionaries are able to go in and harvest souls. When the groundwork is done, hearts are open to receive.

One very effective tool that God has provided is the *Jesus* film, which has travelled to many nations. There have been hundreds of reports of Muslims, Buddhists, and Hindus who have had dreams of Jesus. The Muslims call Him *Isa al Masih,* "The Man in White". Some have had the dream before they saw the *Jesus* film, and then recognized Him when they watched the film. Some have seen the film first and then had the dream.

Here are some testimonies from Campus Crusade for Christ about the dreams and visions God is imparting to his people:

> *Our director, who leads Campus Crusade's work in these countries, directs a radio program that is being broadcast to the entire region. He reports an outstanding phenomenon, one that is well documented. His office has received thousands of letters from Muslims. Many tell of a dream they had: "I saw Jesus. He declared to me, 'I am the way.' " Moved by this compelling dream, they are writing the Campus Crusade's Middle East office to find out just who Jesus is. Once they know, they freely respond!*

> *In Algeria, a number of people discovered they had the very same dream. They began to talk with one another and discovered each had experienced the same dream. The details were the same, and even the words Jesus said to them were the same. On their own, they have formed a Bible study and are following Christ!*

> *A politically active woman had spent four years in prison. While there, she experienced a vision of Jesus in her cell. It profoundly affected her and changed her life forever. She is now on the Campus Crusade staff, totally sold out to reaching her Muslim people for her Savior!*

God is speaking to us in these last days of His great love for people in false religions. Recently I received a Word from the Lord about Islam. Here is a section of that Word:

> *I AM God, who loves them and their children and every life is precious to Me. Therefore, I say to you, PRAY FOR THEIR UNBORN CHILDREN. If you will pray, then out of Islam I will bring a new generation of Christ-worshippers, filled with the Spirit of Elijah from the womb, like John the Baptist. PRAY, that these little children will impart My love to their fathers as I draw the hearts of the fathers to the children. The little children shall lead them.*

You may never be a "missionary" in the traveling sense of the word. However, you may be God's choice as a powerful intercessor! Ask God if He wants you to gather a group to pray the blood of Jesus over a nation of the world. Pray for generations past. Pray for the present leaders. Prepare the way of the Lord to bring lost people visions and dreams, opening the heavenlies to let down the revelation and light of God!

EPILOGUE
...FOR SUCH A TIME AS THIS

We live in an awesome era! Knowledge is multiplying at an incredible rate with electronic technology. We travel the globe easily and quickly. And yet in this time of unprecedented progress, we are seeing the very forces of hell unleashed upon the earth, bringing moral decay and destruction. Life is devalued and society has regressed to narcissism and self-indulgence. And YOU were born....for such a time as this.

Esther was also born for a special time in history. Long before she discovered the purpose for which she was called, Esther was chosen to a royal position simply because of her beauty.

> *The king loved Esther more than all the other women, and she obtained grace and favor in his sight more than all the other virgins; so he set the royal crown upon her head and made her queen instead of Vashti. Esther 2:17*

We, too, have been chosen to live in this era of history for our King of Kings, who has found us lovely and has crowned us with His grace and favor. Like Esther, we must go through a preparation period in which we are made more beautiful and pleasing to our Lord. Esther was bathed for six months in oil of myrrh. In the Hebrew, myrrh means "bitter", and in Greek, "strengthened". We also face bitter circumstances, in order to die to self and be strengthened by the Spirit. Receiving forgiveness, giving forgiveness, dying to our old ways, and embracing emotional healing are our "perfumes" of beautification. We are being prepared for a work that is mightier than we can imagine.

Esther was privileged to live in favorable surroundings. Behind her pleasant environment, however, a wicked plot was being conceived to destroy the Jews, Esther's own people. Likewise, satan has implemented a treacherous plan to destroy our loved ones, to divide our families and implement evil world domination.

When Esther discovered the plot against her people, she gave up all concern for her own personal comfort and safety and dedicated herself to saving her people. She fasted and prayed and conceived a plan. She honored the King, so that she would have favor with him and would be able to implore him to stop the massacre of the Jews.

Esther's heart was aligned with God's heart for His people. Like Jesus, later, she was ready to sacrifice her life to see the people she loved released from satan's assignment. Today, the situation is even more serious, and we are chosen to be Esthers for our generation.

As the world grows darker, God is raising up a powerful army of light-bearers to dispel the darkness. Esther's uncle Mordecai asked this question of her, and I ask this question of you:

> *Yet who knows whether you have come to the kingdom for such a time as this? Esther 4: 14*

Esther's people were delivered from death's door. They conquered their enemies, and rested and celebrated with feasting and gladness.

What is the role of the Church? Meditate a minute on this familiar scripture:

> *For God so loved the world that He gave His only begotten Son, that whosoever believes in Him should not perish but have everlasting life. For God did not send His Son into the world to condemn the world, but that **the world through Him might be saved**.*
> *John 3:16-17*

This does not say that Jesus came just to save the world, but that Jesus came to lay down a path for us... Himself. Therefore, **through Him we would bring restoration to a world the devil had contaminated**.

> *For I consider that the sufferings of this present time are not worthy to be compared with the glory which shall be revealed in us. For the earnest expectation of the creation*

eagerly waits for the revealing of the sons of God. Romans 8: 18-19

Taking back what the devil stole is a supernatural work! It takes people who can operate in the Spirit realm supernaturally to do it. People who can, through Him, shine grace and forgiveness in the face of darkness. The creation has been waiting a long time for that supernatural race of people to be revealed by God!

Beloved, now we are children of God; and it has not yet been revealed what we shall be, but we know that when He is revealed, we shall be like Him, for we shall see Him as He is. I John 3:2

We are those supernatural people that God is revealing and the way we will be recognized is that we will be like Jesus, **unconditionally loving and forgiving as He is**, walking with supernatural authority and anointing ...totally unoffendable!

... to the intent that the manifold wisdom of God might be made known by the Church to the principalities and powers in the heavenly places, according to the eternal purpose which He accomplished in Christ Jesus our Lord. Ephesians 3: 10-11

And there is even more to be accomplished than the restoration of Earth. What goes on in the heavenly realms? Satan, the "accuser", accuses God of foolishness in sending His only Son to be tortured and killed for the sake of human beings who are worthless and evil. But God's manifold (many-faceted) wisdom is being proven to principalities and powers in heavenly places as we, the Church, reveal the power of the Holy Spirit within us because of Jesus' sacrifice on the cross. We endure and persevere **(FORGIVE)** in spite of persecution. We pull down strongholds and take back territory that has been invaded by evil. We build God's Kingdom, one soul at a time, using the power of Christ's blood **(FORGIVENESS).** We are a mighty force on the earth, the Children of God!

Don't minimize your part in this huge move of God in history! If you are living and breathing, then you have been called "for such a time as this" to open heaven and direct the flow of **FORGIVING BLOOD** of Jesus to your family, your neighbors, your city, and your world!

APPENDIX

FORGIVENESS PRAYERS

Lord, I come humbly to You, knowing that I have failed to love others as You have loved me, and asking forgiveness for all of my failures, my weaknesses and mistakes, my wrong attitudes and wrong decisions, and for every action I have taken that has caused harm to others. I receive Your forgiveness now. Out of obedience and a grateful heart, I choose to cancel the debts of all persons who have harmed me, to drop all offenses and give each one into Your care for Your blessing.

Lord, I have made a nesting place in my heart for Your Spirit. Come now and inhabit me. I commit myself totally to Your will and service.

Thank you for the authority you have given to me. At the name of Jesus, every knee shall bow, of things in heaven and things of earth and things under the earth, and that every tongue shall confess that Jesus Christ is Lord, to the glory of God the Father. Whatever I bind on earth through unforgiveness shall be bound in heaven and whatever I loose on earth through forgiveness shall be loosed in heaven.

I renounce all fellowship with satan and the occult and break all power of satan and his demons over my life. Forgive me, Lord, if I have been involved in any occult practices. Thank you, Lord, for Your protection from satanic interference, as I proceed with forgiveness and deliverance in Jesus' name.

Lord, if I have blamed You for anything that has happened in my life, I ask You to forgive me. I know that You are not the author of confusion or disaster, but that You love me with an everlasting love, and You make sure that all things work together for my good.

GENERATIONS PAST

Lord, I lift up my relatives from past generations. On behalf of myself and my entire family, I repent of all our iniquities. I ask You to forgive all of our sin. I break every curse and spell passed down to us, and I break the power of all familiar spirits that have come down the family line. I apply the blood of Jesus on the bloodline of our family, cleansing, healing and setting this family free of all physical and mental diseases, iniquities and breaking all bondages. I break the power of all spirits of unforgiveness, judgment, condemnation, and accusation in Jesus' name.

MYSELF

Lord, I choose to forgive myself for all my faults and shortcomings, for all my sins, mistakes, bad judgments, unwise actions and for my lack of love. I forgive myself for any word curses or vows I have spoken against myself, and I break their power now. I forgive myself now for anything that you bring to my mind at this time. Bless me to the fullness of Your grace.

MOTHER

Thank you, Lord, for the one who birthed me into this world. I forgive her of lack of love, lack of attention or neglect or negative feelings shown toward me. I forgive her for words spoken that shamed me or spoke negative things into my life. I forgive her for abandonment, or rejection, or choosing others over me. I forgive her for anything You are bringing to mind right now. Bless her to the fullness of Your grace.

I forgive any foster mother or adoptive mother of harmful actions or attitudes that hurt me, and for anything You are bringing to mind right now. Bless her to the fullness of Your grace.

FATHER

Lord, I forgive my father for lack of attention or involvement with my upbringing, for lack in caring for the family, for any selfishness on his part that left others in the family feeling rejected and unloved, for abandonment or betrayal. I forgive him for anything You are revealing to me at this moment. Bless him to the fullness of Your grace.

I forgive any foster father or adoptive father of harmful actions or attitudes that hurt me, and for anything You are bringing to mind right now. Bless him to the fullness of Your grace.

SIBLINGS

Lord, I forgive my brothers and sisters for their jealousy, not doing their part, not sharing, for selfishness, and for lack of consideration toward me. In every way that they brought harm to me, I forgive, and for anything that You are revealing to me right now. Bless them to the fullness of Your grace.

HUSBAND

I forgive my husband, Lord, for any qualities that he has lacked as a husband, for things that he has said that have deeply hurt me, for putting other things before my welfare, for lack of compassion or understanding and for poor communication. I forgive him for every action that brought disunity in our family, and for any other thing that You are showing me now. Bless him to the fullness of Your grace.

I forgive my ex-husband(s) for his faults, failures, bad attitudes, and whatever You bring to my mind right now. Bless him to the fullness of Your grace.

PAST UNGODLY RELATIONSHIPS

Lord, you have forgiven me of my sins, including any sexual sins of the past, fornication or adultery. I forgive each person with whom I have had an ungodly relationship. I break the soul tie with each and every one. Lead me in this now.

Lord, I also choose to forgive every person who has taken advantage of me against my will, raped me, or performed perverted sexual acts upon me, either as an adult or as a child. I break the soul tie with this (these) person(s). I trust You to take my pain and to bring inner healing to my soul as I am obedient to You and voice with my mouth the desire to forgive. Bless each one to the fullness of Your grace.

CHILDREN

I forgive my children for lack of appreciation, rebellion against authority, lack of understanding and compassion, selfishness, bad behavior, addictions, laziness, lack of interest in God and all actions harmful to themselves or others. I also forgive whatever You reveal to me now. Bless them to the fullness of Your grace.

RELATIVES

Lord, I forgive my aunts, uncles, cousins, grandparents, and relatives by marriage that have been difficult to get along with, interfering in my family affairs, or distant and withdrawn when they were needed. I also forgive them of whatever You are showing me now. Bless them to the fullness of Your grace.

BOSSES AND CO-WORKERS

I forgive my boss and past bosses for their unfair or harsh treatment, lack of appreciation for my work, unwillingness to pay a fair wage, and for prejudice and partiality toward the workers.

I forgive my co-workers, past and present, of not doing their share, making themselves look good by putting me down, gossiping about me or any other behavior that has hurt me.

I also forgive them of whatever You are showing me now. Bless them to the fullness of Your grace.

NEIGHBORS

Lord, I forgive my neighbors for being too noisy or too interfering, or inconsiderate in their behavior, or ill mannered toward me or my family, and also for anything that You show me at this time. Bless them to the fullness of Your grace.

FRIENDS

I forgive my friends, Lord, who abandoned me when I needed them, or gossiped about me behind my back, or accused me or lied to me and did not try to work things out, or borrowed my things and did not give them back. I also forgive them of whatever You bring to mind now. Bless them to the fullness of Your grace.

CHURCH

Lord, I forgive my church for not being there for me when I needed them, for not understanding my situation and judging me or my family, for religiosity and legalism and for false or misguided teaching. I forgive my pastor for anything he has done to hurt me, or neglected to do that caused me to feel rejected. I also forgive them of whatever You bring to mind now. Bless them to the fullness of Your grace.

THOSE WITH DIFFERENT BELIEFS

I forgive all of those people in my life who have different political, religious, or cultural belief systems who have judged me inferior, given me a hard time, or caused embarrassment, humiliation and harm. I forgive them also for anything You bring to mind, Lord. Bless them to the fullness of Your grace.

PROFESSIONALS

Lord, I forgive all doctors, nurses, lawyers, judges, juries, policemen, firemen, store owners and personnel, construction workers, repairmen, or any others who have treated me without consideration, unfairly, and harmfully. I also forgive any others that You bring to my mind now. Bless them to the fullness of Your grace.

TEACHERS

I forgive all those who were entrusted with the responsibility of teaching me, who abused their authority to put me down or embarrass me, to physically harm me, to treat me unfairly or punished me too harshly. I also forgive them of any other things You bring to my mind. Bless them to the fullness of Your grace.

Thank you, Lord, that I am completely clean, forgiven, and freed from the sin of unforgiveness, in Jesus' precious name, amen.

REFERENCES AND RESOURCES

Bright, Bill. (1996) Campus Crusade for Christ Newsletter

Burns, Lauretta P. *"Broken Dreams".*
(http://www.raindrop.org/rain/poets/chr18.shtml)

Chambers, Oswald. (1992) **My Utmost for His Highest**.
Bloomington, Minnesota: Garbarg's Heart 'n Home, Inc.

Cloud, Henry and John Townsend. (1992). **Boundaries.**
Grand Rapids, Michigan: Zondervan.

Cloud, Henry and John Townsend. (1995). **Safe People.**
Grand Rapids, Michigan: Zondervan.

Cole, Edwin Louis. (1982). **Maximized Manhood: A Guide
to Family Survival,** Springdale, Pennsylvania: Whitaker
House. P. 54.

Garlington, Joseph. (1994) "Intercessors or Judges?"
Charisma Magazine. (June, P. 12.)

Jacobs, Cindy. (1991). **Possessing the Gates of the Enemy.**
Tarrytown, New York: Rev. Fleming H. Nevell Co.

King, Martin Luther Jr. *Martin Luther King, Jr. Quotes.*
(http://brainyquote.com/quotes/authors/m/martin_
luther_king_jr.html)

McGee, Robert and Dawson McAllister. (1990). **Search for
Significance** (Youth Edition). Irving, Texas: Shepherd
Ministries.

McGinnis, Sylvia. (2013). **Would You Believe**. Kerrville,
Texas: Restoration Ministries.

Nee, Watchman. (1965). **The Release of the Spirit.**
Indianapolis, Indiana: Sure Foundation.

Peterson, Eugene H. (2002). **The Message Bible.** Colorado Springs, Colorado: NavPress Publishing Group.

Powers, Marie. (1996). **Shame: Thief of Intimacy.** Edmonds, Washington. Aglow International.

The NKJV-Amplified Parallel Bible. (2013) Peabody, Massachusetts: Hendrickson Publishers Marketing, LLC.

The New Open Bible. (1990). New King James Version. Nashville, Tennessee: Thomas Nelson Publishers.

The New Strong's Exhaustive Concordance of the Bible. (1984). Nashville, Tennessee: Thomas Nelson Publishers.

Townsend, John. (2011). **Beyond Boundaries.** Grand Rapids, Michigan: Zondervan.

Smith, Ed M. **Beyond Tolerable Recovery.** Campbellsville, Kentucky: Family Care Publishing.

Wagner, C. Peter. (1996). "A Season of Reconciliation." **Charisma Magazine,** (March, pp. 60-63).

Webster's Seventh New Collegiate Dictionary. (1971). Springfield, Massachusetts: G&C Merriam Co.

Wesley, Charles. "Love Divine, All Loves Excelling." (1980). **Hymns of Faith**. Wheaton, Illinois: Tabernacle Publishing Company

Wigglesworth, Smith. (1998) **Smith Wiggleswoth on Spiritual Gifts**. New Kensington, Pennsylvania: Whitaker House.

To order more copies of this book
or
Sylvia McGinnis' previous book entitled

WOULD YOU BELIEVE...
A PERSONAL GUIDE TO INNER HEALING

Contact the author at:

sylviamcginnis@hotmail.com

.

www.ingramcontent.com/pod-product-compliance
Lightning Source LLC
LaVergne TN
LVHW051055080426

835508LV00019B/1897